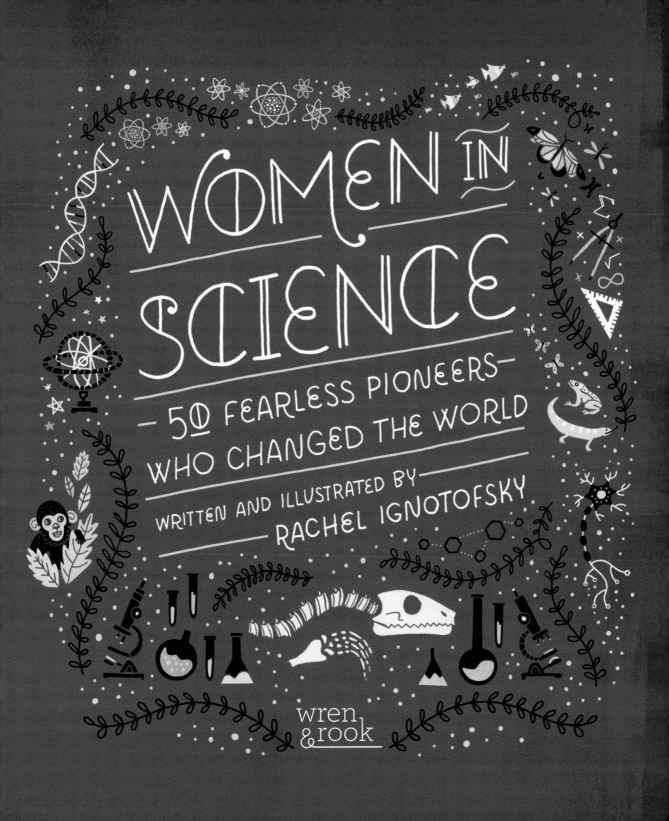

WOMEN IN SCIENCE

— 50 FEARLESS PIONEERS —
WHO CHANGED THE WORLD

WRITTEN AND ILLUSTRATED BY
RACHEL IGNOTOFSKY

wren
&rook

CONTENTS

INTRODUCTION

Nothing says trouble like a woman in trousers. That was the attitude in the 1930s, anyway; when Barbara McClintock wore chinos at the University of Missouri, it was considered scandalous. Even worse, she was feisty, direct, incredibly smart and twice as sharp as most of her male colleagues. If you think these seem like good qualities for a scientist, you're right. But back then, these weren't necessarily considered good qualities in a woman.

Barbara made her mark on the field of genetics with her pioneering work mapping chromosomes. Yet while working at the University of Missouri, Barbara was seen as bold and unladylike. The faculty excluded her from meetings and gave her little support. When she found out that they would fire her if she got married and there was no possibility of promotion, she packed her bags. With no plan, except an unwillingness to compromise her worth, Barbara went to find her dream job. This decision would allow her to eventually make the discovery of jumping genes, winning her a Nobel Prize and forever changing how we view genetics.

Barbara McClintock's story is not unique. As long as humanity has asked questions about our world, men and women have looked to the stars, under rocks and through microscopes to find the answers. Both men and women have the same thirst for knowledge, but women have not always been given the same opportunities to explore the answers.

In the past, restrictions on women's access to education were not uncommon. Women were often not allowed to publish scientific papers. They were expected to grow up to become good wives and mothers while their husbands provided for them. Many people thought women were just not as smart as men. The women in this book had to fight these stereotypes to have the careers they wanted. They broke rules, published under pseudonyms and worked for the love of learning alone. When others doubted their abilities, they had to believe in themselves.

When women finally began gaining wider access to higher education, there was usually a catch. Often they would be given no space to work, no funding and no recognition. Not allowed to enter the university building, Lise Meitner did her radiochemistry experiments in a dank basement. Without funding for a lab, Marie Curie handled dangerous radioactive elements in a tiny, dusty shed. After making one of the most important discoveries in astronomy, Cecilia Payne-Gaposchkin worked for decades as a technical assistant. Creativity, persistence and a love of discovery were the greatest tools these women had.

Marie Curie is now a household name, but throughout history there have been many other great and important women in the fields of science, technology, engineering and mathematics. Many did not receive the recognition they deserved at the time and were forgotten. When thinking of physics, we should name not only Albert Einstein but also Emmy Noether. We should all know that it was Rosalind Franklin who discovered the double helix structure of DNA, not James Watson and Francis Crick. While admiring the advances in computer technology, let us remember not only Steve Jobs or Bill Gates, but also Grace Hopper.

Throughout history many women have risked everything in the name of science. This book tells the stories of some of these scientists, who in the face of 'No' said, 'Try and stop me.'

ONE OF THE FIRST RECORDED WOMEN TO STUDY & TEACH MATHS.

HAS BECOME A SYMBOL FOR ENLIGHTENMENT AND FEMINISM.

AN EXPERT IN PHILOSOPHY, ASTRONOMY AND MATHEMATICS.

'IN SPEECH ARTICULATE AND LOGICAL, IN HER ACTIONS PRUDENT AND PUBLIC-SPIRITED ... THE CITY GAVE HER SUITABLE WELCOME AND ACCORDED HER SPECIAL RESPECT.' —THE *SUDA LEXICON*

HYPATIA

ASTRONOMER, MATHEMATICIAN AND PHILOSOPHER

Hypatia was one of the earliest recorded female mathematicians. Her accomplishments in life inspired many, but her death turned her into a legend.

Hypatia was born between 350 and 370 CE in Alexandria, Egypt. Her father, Theon, was a famous scholar. He made sure that she was well educated and that she grew up with a deep respect for their Greek heritage and values.

Alexandria, known for its library, was a great place of learning – but it was also rife with religious tensions between pagans, Jews and Christians that could turn violent. This made it dangerous for Hypatia and her father to practise their Greek traditions.

Her father instructed her in mathematics and astronomy, and she became an expert in both. Soon she surpassed her father and produced important commentary on his mathematical work, while making her own contributions to geometry and number theory. Hypatia was also an expert in platonic philosophy. She was one of Alexandria's first female teachers. People travelled from faraway lands to hear her speak! Her male students gave her respect and loyalty.

Eventually the brewing religious tensions in the area turned violent, and Hypatia's 'pagan' teachings made her a target. She was killed around 415 CE by extremist Christians. Although her death was a tragedy, her life has become a symbol for education in the face of ignorance. We remember Hypatia as a source of light and knowledge.

THE WISEST

HER FATHER WAS ONE OF THE LAST MEMBERS OF THE LIBRARY OF ALEXANDRIA.

INVENTED A NEW VERSION OF THE HYDROMETER.

SHE IS DEPICTED IN RAPHAEL'S FAMOUS PAINTING 'THE SCHOOL OF ATHENS'.

IS CITED IN AN ANCIENT ENCYCLOPAEDIA CALLED THE SUDA.

WAS KNOWN AS 'THE EGYPTIAN WISE WOMAN'.

THE LIBRARY OF ALEXANDRIA ENDURED WARS & REVOLTS. IT WAS DESTROYED IN 391 CE, WHEN THE ROMAN EMPIRE OUTLAWED PAGANISM.

WORKED WITH HER FATHER ON THEORIES ABOUT THE SOLAR SYSTEM.

MADE PUBLIC SPEECHES ABOUT PLATO & ARISTOTLE.

ONE OF THE FIRST AND MOST IMPORTANT ENTOMOLOGISTS.

CLASSIFIED MANY NEW INSECT SPECIES.

CAREFULLY ILLUSTRATED THE METAMORPHOSIS OF THE BUTTERFLY.

'ART AND NATURE SHALL ALWAYS BE WRESTLING UNTIL THEY EVENTUALLY CONQUER ONE ANOTHER SO THAT THE VICTORY IS THE STROKE AND LINE.' — MARIA SIBYLLA MERIAN

MARIA SIBYLLA MERIAN

SCIENTIFIC ILLUSTRATOR AND ENTOMOLOGIST

Born in Germany in 1647, Maria Sibylla Merian combined science and art to become one of the great scientific illustrators of history.

In the 1600s, most people thought insects were disgusting and not worth careful study. Maria could not have disagreed more. At a young age she started collecting insects to learn how they behaved. She painted the different stages of her favourite insects' lives.

Maria was particularly interested in butterflies. At the time, no one really understood the connection between caterpillars and butterflies. In 1679, she published a book on metamorphosis, filled with scientific notes and illustrations.

Then Maria's life changed drastically. She left her husband and took her mother and two daughters to Holland. They joined a strict religious group with ties to a Dutch colony in South America called Suriname. The group fell apart, but Maria's interest in Suriname stayed. Aged 52, she braved its rainforests to document never-before-seen bugs. Her trip ended early when she contracted malaria, but she had all she needed to create her greatest book. *The Metamorphosis of the Insects of Suriname* was published in 1705 and became a hit all over Europe.

Maria's detailed illustrations amaze people to this day.

PEOPLE THOUGHT MARIA LOVED BUGS BECAUSE HER MUM VISITED AN INSECT COLLECTION WHILE PREGNANT.

PEOPLE USED TO CALL INSECTS 'THE BEASTS OF THE DEVIL'.

MARIA OBSERVED & PAINTED LIVE INSECTS WHILE OTHERS OBSERVED ONLY DEAD ONES IN DISPLAY CASES.

PEOPLE USED TO THINK INSECTS WOULD SPONTANEOUSLY APPEAR IN RUBBISH LIKE MAGIC.

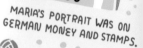

MARIA'S PORTRAIT WAS ON GERMAN MONEY AND STAMPS.

COCOONS WERE ONCE CALLED 'DATE PITS' IN GERMANY.

SHE HANDLED POISONOUS BUGS IN THE RAINFOREST.

WROTE POLITICAL POETRY ABOUT INJUSTICE.

WROTE PAPERS EXPLAINING TRIGONOMETRY AND THE PRINCIPLES OF MULTIPLICATION AND DIVISION.

ACCURATELY RECORDED LUNAR ECLIPSES & EQUINOXES.

'IT'S MADE TO BELIEVE/WOMEN ARE THE SAME AS MEN;/ARE YOU NOT CONVINCED/DAUGHTERS CAN ALSO BE HEROIC?'— WANG ZHENYI'S POETRY

WANG ZHENYI

★ ASTRONOMER, POET <u>AND</u> MATHEMATICIAN ★

Wang Zhenyi was one of the greatest scholars in China. She was born in 1768 during the Qing dynasty. At the time, education was only for the wealthy and women were not expected to 'bother' with studies.

Fortunately, Wang Zhenyi was born into a family of scholars who valued her education. Her grandfather and father taught her astronomy and maths. She also travelled extensively and learned about the harshness of poverty, inspiring her to write poetry decrying injustice.

In Wang Zhenyi's day, eclipses were not well understood. But she had theories about how they worked, and she created her own eclipse model using a mirror, a lamp and a globe. Wang Zhenyi used it to prove her theories about how the Moon blocks our view of the Sun – or the Earth blocks the Sun's light from reaching the Moon – during an eclipse. She also scientifically studied the Chinese calendar system and used her telescope to measure the stars and further explain the rotation of the solar system.

Wang Zhenyi was also a dedicated mathematician. She understood complicated arithmetic theories and at the age of 24 published a five-volume guide for beginners called *Simple Principles of Calculation*.

Wang Zhenyi only lived to the age of 29, yet she is remembered as a great mind of the Qing dynasty. She published many books on maths, astronomy and poetry, and her work influenced legions of scientists who came after her.

LOVED HER GRANDFATHER'S HUGE LIBRARY OF BOOKS.

UNDERSTOOD THAT THE EARTH WAS ROUND AND DESCRIBED IT AS A BALL.

LEARNED FROM WESTERN & EASTERN CALENDARS.

WAS ACCOMPLISHED IN ARCHERY & HORSEBACK RIDING.

EXPLAINED ECLIPSES IN HER PAPER 'THE DISPUTE OF THE PROCESSION OF THE EQUINOXES'.

UPDATED THE COUNT AND PLACEMENT OF THE STARS.

DEVELOPED HER OWN ARGUMENTS ON GRAVITY.

WROTE COMMENTARIES ON THE PYTHAGOREAN THEOREM AND OTHER TRIGONOMETRIC STUDIES.

$$a^2 + b^2 = c^2$$

MARY ANNING

FOSSIL COLLECTOR AND PALAEONTOLOGIST

Mary Anning was born in 1799 in a small English seaside town called Lyme Regis. Her family was very poor, so she helped her father collect fossils to sell to tourists. It was dangerous work because the cliffs were steep, yet 11-year-old Mary took over the fossil business when her father died.

There was a time when people had never heard of dinosaurs and thought it was impossible for a species to go extinct. Mary helped to prove this wrong. When she was 12, she found the first complete ichthyosaur skeleton. She went on to discover two skeletons of the previously unknown species plesiosaur. These fossils were unlike any living animal, proving that extinction could occur. She also discovered the first pterosaur skeleton outside of Germany and many ancient fossilised fish. She helped determine that stones called bezoars were actually fossilised poo!

Mary was not allowed to publish work because she was a woman. Male doctors and geologists respected her ideas and used her findings in their own work, but her name was edited out. Although this was unfair, it was remarkable that a working-class woman was allowed to mingle with educated men in Victorian Britain.

Mary Anning's discoveries let the world see fossils as more than mystical oddities.

HER DOG 'TRAY' CAME WITH HER ON FOSSIL DIGS UNTIL HE DIED IN A LANDSLIDE.

SHE SOLD FOSSILS TO NOBLE GENTLEMEN.

HER LIFE INSPIRED MANY MODERN FICTIONAL STORIES.

FOSSILS

THERE IS A MYTH THAT HER GENIUS CAME FROM BEING STRUCK BY LIGHTNING AS A CHILD.

IT'S RUMOURED THAT THE TONGUE-TWISTER 'SHE SELLS SEA SHELLS' IS ABOUT MARY ANNING.

PEOPLE CALLED FOSSILS 'DEVILS TOENAILS' AND SNAKE STONES.

WAS THE FIRST PERSON TO CREATE A COMPUTER PROGRAM.

WROTE ONE OF THE MOST IMPORTANT DOCUMENTS IN COMPUTER HISTORY.

IS HONOURED WITH ADA LOVELACE DAY.

'IMAGINATION IS THE DISCOVERING FACULTY, PRE-EMINENTLY. IT IS THAT WHICH PENETRATES INTO THE UNSEEN WORLDS AROUND US, THE WORLDS OF SCIENCE.' — ADA LOVELACE

ADA LOVELACE

MATHEMATICIAN AND WRITER

When Ada Lovelace first saw the Difference Engine, she became obsessed. The early computing pioneer Charles Babbage invented this gigantic, gear-filled calculator and, after meeting him in 1833, Ada convinced him to work with her.

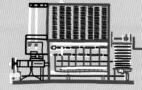

Ada's mother, Anne Isabella Milbanke, was a mathematician who wanted the right upbringing for her daughter. Ada's father was the famed poet Lord Byron. The wildness that made him an amazing poet also made Byron a lousy husband, which led Anne to leave him after Ada was born. Ada was given an unusually strict mathematical education.

Ada met Charles Babbage when she was 17 and very persistent. She begged him to take her on as a student, but he was much too busy. So when Ada saw a French article about his newest idea, the Analytical Engine, she saw her chance to impress him. She translated the paper into English and published it in 1843. But that wasn't all; she added her own notes, making it twice as long! This got Charles's attention, and their collaboration began.

Ada imagined a world where computers did more than calculations – where they could write music and become extensions of human thought. She also designed a way to program the Analytical Engine, using punch cards with a sequence of rational numbers. It was the first computer program ever!

Ada remains an inspiration to this day. Her name has become proof that women can accomplish great things in technology, computing and programming.

- SHE DESCRIBED HERSELF AS A POETICAL SCIENTIST.

- HER LAST NAME COMES FROM HER HUSBAND, WILLIAM KING, THE EARL OF LOVELACE.

- ADA LOVELACE DAY IS CELEBRATED ON THE 2nd TUESDAY IN OCTOBER.

- SHE HAS INSPIRED CHARACTERS IN NARRATIVE & GRAPHIC NOVELS.

- THE US DEPARTMENT OF DEFENSE NAMED A COMPUTER LANGUAGE 'ADA'.

- SHE SIGNED HER LETTERS TO CHARLES BABBAGE AS 'LADY FAIRY'.

- HER PROGRAM WAS INSPIRED BY THE PUNCH CARDS USED IN MECHANICAL LOOMS.

WORKED WITH THE POOR TO FIGHT SOCIAL INJUSTICE WITH MEDICINE.

FIRST WOMAN IN AMERICA TO RECEIVE A MEDICAL DEGREE.

FOUNDED THE NEW YORK INFIRMARY FOR WOMEN AND CHILDREN, AND THE LONDON SCHOOL OF MEDICINE FOR WOMEN.

'IF THE PRESENT ARRANGEMENTS OF SOCIETY WILL NOT ADMIT OF

ELIZABETH BLACKWELL

DOCTOR

Elizabeth Blackwell had no interest in medicine until a friend died from uterine cancer. Her friend said she might have experienced less pain and suffering if she had had a female doctor. This put Elizabeth on the path to becoming the first female medical doctor in the United States. She was mentored by male doctor friends and read books from their libraries. Defying all expectations, she was accepted into Geneva Medical College.

Elizabeth had to sit separately from the male students, and her teachers were embarrassed by her presence during anatomy lessons. When asked to leave a lecture about reproduction, she argued her way into staying. During the summer she worked in a Philadelphia hospital and saw how its conditions contributed to the spread of infectious disease. This inspired her thesis on how good hygiene can prevent the spread of typhus. In 1849, she graduated first in her class.

Elizabeth's sister Emily also became a doctor. With Dr Marie Zakrzewska, they opened the New York Infirmary for Indigent Women and Children in 1857. They treated the poor and taught female medical students and nurses.

In the 1800s, there was little known about contagious disease. It was common for doctors to go from treating a flu patient to delivering a baby without washing their hands, causing the spread of diseases. Elizabeth called for better hygiene standards in hospitals and homes.

Elizabeth went on to found the Women's Medical College of the New York Infirmary in 1868, and the London School of Medicine for Women around 1874. An inspiration to many, she made it possible for women to become doctors.

HA HA

SHE WAS ACCEPTED INTO MEDICAL SCHOOL WHEN THE STUDENT BODY VOTED YES, AS A PRACTICAL JOKE: SHE SHOWED UP ANYWAY.

WAS A PROFESSOR OF GYNAECOLOGY AT THE LONDON SCHOOL OF MEDICINE FOR WOMEN.

ADVOCATED FOR WOMEN'S RIGHTS, ESPECIALLY EQUAL OPPORTUNITY FOR FEMALE DOCTORS.

WROTE MANY BOOKS & PAPERS ON PUBERTY, PARENTING AND FAMILY PLANNING.

TRAINED IN PARIS AND LONDON MATERNITY WARDS AFTER MEDICAL SCHOOL.

I CAN NEVER BE A SURGEON NOW.

IN 1849, WHILE CARING FOR A BABY'S GONORRHOEA-INFECTED EYE, ELIZABETH BECAME INFECTED HERSELF & LOST SIGHT IN ONE EYE.

HELPED TRAIN UNION NURSES WITH HER SISTER DURING THE CIVIL WAR.

STARTED THE NATIONAL HEALTH SOCIETY IN LONDON.

FIRST WOMAN TO WIN A HUGHES MEDAL FROM THE ROYAL SOCIETY IN THE UK.

INVENTED A BETTER ELECTRIC ARC AND FURTHERED OUR UNDERSTANDING OF ELECTRICAL CURRENT.

FIRST WOMAN ACCEPTED INTO THE INSTITUTION OF ELECTRICAL ENGINEERS.

'AN ERROR THAT ASCRIBES TO A MAN WHAT WAS ACTUALLY THE WORK OF A WOMAN HAS MORE LIVES THAN A CAT.' – HERTHA AYRTON

HERTHA AYRTON

ENGINEER, MATHEMATICIAN AND INVENTOR

REGISTERED 26 PATENTS.

In 1854, Phoebe Sarah Marks was born in Britain. She was so energetic that her friends nicknamed her Hertha – after a German Earth goddess – a name she liked so much that she adopted it.

Hertha's family was poor, so at 16 she became a governess. There she met Madame Bodichon, a leader of the suffragist movement, who paid for Hertha's education. In technical school, she met Professor William Ayrton, who became her husband and partner in invention.

GIRL POWER

WAS GOOD FRIENDS WITH MARIE CURIE.

STUDIED WIND MOTION AND WATER VORTICES.

In the 1890s, hissing electric arcs were used for streetlights. William and Hertha wanted to improve the technology. One day, while William was away, Hertha invented a new arc that made a quiet bright light.

Hertha burst open doors for women by getting published and giving lectures on electricity. During demonstrations about the arc, people were amazed to see a woman wielding such dangerous-looking equipment! She was the first female member of the Institution of Electrical Engineers, but she was still not allowed to speak at the Royal Society. However, when her book *The Electric Arc* was published in 1902, it became too successful to ignore – the Royal Society let her present a paper. In 1906, they awarded her the Hughes Medal for her work on electricity.

Hertha was also a vocal advocate of the suffragist movement and provided aid to women on hunger strikes. In Britain's 1911 census, she wrote an impassioned letter on the form, demanding votes for women!

Hertha's genius paved the way for women to play with 'dangerous' machinery and invent great things.

NAMED HER CHILD AFTER MADAME BARBARA BODICHON, HER FRIEND & SUPPORTER.

WAS THE FIRST WOMAN NOMINATED TO BE A FELLOW OF THE ROYAL SOCIETY

(THOUGH THEY DID NOT OFFICIALLY ACCEPT WOMEN UNTIL THE 1940s).

INVENTED THE AYRTON FAN TO BLOW AWAY MUSTARD GAS DURING WORLD WAR I.

INVENTED A LINE DIVIDER FOR ARCHITECTS.

CREATED A NEW THEORY OF NEUROSIS TO HELP PEOPLE COPE WITH ANXIETY.

HELPED CREATE A NEW FIELD OF PSYCHOLOGY CALLED NEO-FREUDIANISM.

DEVELOPED THE FOUNDATIONS OF FEMINIST PSYCHOLOGY.

NEUROSIS AND HUMAN GROWTH

'FORTUNATELY ANALYSIS IS NOT THE ONLY WAY TO RESOLVE INNER CONFLICTS. LIFE ITSELF STILL REMAINS A VERY EFFECTIVE THERAPIST.' — KAREN HORNEY

KAREN HORNEY

PSYCHOANALYST

In the early 1900s, psychology emerged as a new social science that researched how the mind worked. Sigmund Freud was the father of psychoanalytic theory. His ideas focused mainly on male minds and argued that women wished they were men.

Karen Horney was born in Germany in 1885 and earned her medical degree at the University of Berlin. Her own battles with depression inspired her to study psychology. She began teaching at the Berlin Psychoanalytic Institute in 1920. Through her many clinical studies, she observed behaviour that did not fit Freudian theory, leading her to rebel against it.

Karen argued that society didn't allow women to have any real power but instead forced them to live through their husbands and children. She theorised that women didn't want to become men; they just wanted the independence that men had. She argued that society shapes a person's perception of self-worth. In doing this, she created the field of feminist psychology.

Karen moved to America in 1932 and worked at the New School for Social Research and the New York Psychoanalytic Institute. There, she created a new theory of anxiety, arguing that it is not just caused by our biology but also by the environment in which we grow up. It directly contradicted Freud's theories and Karen faced a fierce backlash, which eventually forced her out of the New York Psychoanalytic Institute in 1941. She continued to write many books and founded the Association for the Advancement of Psychoanalysis.

Karen Horney created a new way of thinking about ourselves, society and anxiety. She is still considered one of the most influential psychologists ever.

HER MENTOR, KARL ABRAHAM, WAS A SUPER CLOSE FRIEND OF FREUD'S.

FOUNDED THE AMERICAN JOURNAL OF PSYCHOANALYSIS.

FOUNDED THE AMERICAN INSTITUTE FOR PSYCHOANALYSIS & BECAME THE DEAN!

SHE WROTE MANY BOOKS INCLUDING THE POPULAR THE NEUROTIC PERSONALITY OF OUR TIME.

INSPIRED THE TERM 'WOMB ENVY'!

THE HORNEY CLINIC IN NEW YORK IS NAMED AFTER HER.

DISCOVERED THAT SEX IS DETERMINED BY 'X' AND 'Y' CHROMOSOMES.

ONE OF THE FIRST WOMEN IN AMERICA TO BE RECOGNISED FOR HER BIOLOGY RESEARCH.

CHANGED HOW WE STUDY EMBRYOS AND CYTOGENETICS.

'MISS STEVENS HAD A SHARE IN A DISCOVERY OF IMPORTANCE, AND HER WORK WILL BE REMEMBERED FOR THIS.' —THOMAS HUNT MORGAN

NETTIE STEVENS

GENETICIST

Nettie Stevens was born in 1861 in Vermont, USA. She pinched pennies to pay for her education and often taught classes to help pay her way. Nettie finished her undergrad education at Stanford University and received her PhD at Bryn Mawr College at the age of 41.

The big question in genetics at the time was a simple one: what makes a baby a girl or a boy? For centuries, doctors had thought a baby's sex was determined by what a woman ate during pregnancy or how warm she kept her body. Nettie and other scientists thought that there was more to sex determination than that.

Nettie got to work by dissecting bugs. She took sex organs from butterflies and mealworms to look at under a microscope. She found male insects had an XY-shaped chromosome but females had an XX. In 1905, she published her groundbreaking research in a two-part book, which overturned centuries of misconceptions.

Around the same time, Edmund Wilson, Nettie's former advisor, made the same discovery of XY chromosomes. Nettie's work had the strongest proof and she wrote about her findings with great scientific conviction, but it was received by a sceptical public and Edmund was awarded the Nobel Prize. Unfortunately, Nettie's untimely death in 1912 rendered her largely overlooked and forgotten. But today we recognise her amazing work, which allowed scientists to understand sex determination and genetics.

SHE ALSO USED FRUIT FLIES & BEETLES IN HER STUDIES.

HER DAD WAS A CARPENTER.

HER HISTORIC WORK WAS CALLED STUDIES IN SPERMATOGENESIS.

TRAVELLED TO ITALY AND GERMANY TO STUDY CYTOLOGY.

TO MAKE SURE THEIR BABY WOULD BE A BOY, PEOPLE USED TO TRY TO CONCEIVE IN THE SUMMER (IT DIDN'T WORK).

NOBEL PRIZE WINNER THOMAS MORGAN'S WORK WAS POSSIBLE BECAUSE OF NETTIE'S RESEARCH.

FIRST WOMAN TO WORK FOR THE U.S GEOLOGICAL SURVEY.

TRAINED ALMOST EVERY FEMALE GEOLOGIST OF HER TIME.

WAS AN EXPERT ON THE PIEDMONT PLATEAU.

'I HAVE CONSIDERABLE PRIDE IN THE FACT THAT SOME OF THE BEST WORK DONE IN GEOLOGY TODAY

FLORENCE BASCOM

GEOLOGIST AND EDUCATOR

FIRST WOMAN OFFICER OF THE GEOLOGIC SOCIETY OF AMERICA.

Florence Bascom was born in Massachusetts, USA in 1862. Florence's father always encouraged her education, and it was a road trip with him and a geologist friend that sparked her interest in rocks.

In 1893, Florence was the first woman to get a PhD from Johns Hopkins University, but it did not come easily. She was forced to take her classes behind a screen so she wouldn't 'distract' her male classmates. Despite the unfair treatment, she became the second woman in America to complete a geology doctorate.

Florence became an authority on rocks and how to categorise them through their chemical make-up and mineral content. In her dissertation, Florence's expertise allowed her to prove that a layer of rock everyone had thought was sedimentary was actually caused by lava flows.

Florence began teaching at Bryn Mawr College in 1895. She trained almost every female geologist in America until she retired in 1928. She was a rigorous teacher but was also able to do important field work for the US Geological Survey. At Bryn Mawr, she began her intensive work in geomorphology, the study of how the Earth's geography changes over thousands of years. Florence's research focused on the hilly area of the Appalachians. She created important geographical maps of New Jersey and Pennsylvania that are still used today.

Florence Bascom rocked the world of geology! Her discoveries and maps continue to influence the field.

FIRST WOMAN OFFICER OF THE GEOLOGIC SOCIETY OF AMERICA.

ROCKS!

ASSOCIATE EDITOR OF THE AMERICAN GEOLOGIST.

WORKED IN A STORAGE SPACE WHERE SHE COLLECTED FOSSILS & ROCKS.

RECEIVED 4 STARS IN THE FIRST EDITION OF AMERICAN MEN OF SCIENCE IN 1906.

SHE STUDIED PHILADELPHIA'S WATER RESOURCES.

PUBLISHED OVER 40 SCIENTIFIC PAPERS.

HELPED INFORM THE MODERN UNDERSTANDING OF HOW MOUNTAINS FORM.

PIONEERED RESEARCH ON RADIOACTIVITY.

WON TWO NOBEL PRIZES.

FOUNDED THE CURIE INSTITUTE IN PARIS.

DISCOVERED 2 ELEMENTS: POLONIUM AND RADIUM.

'I WAS TAUGHT THAT THE WAY OF PROGRESS IS NEITHER SWIFT NOR EASY.' — MARIE CURIE

MARIE CURIE

PHYSICIST AND CHEMIST

FIRST WOMAN TO GET A DOCTORATE IN FRANCE.

POLONIUM WAS NAMED AFTER POLAND.

RADIUM WAS NAMED AFTER THE SUN.

MOTHER OF 2 GIRLS.

FIRST WOMAN TO BE HONOURED FOR HER OWN ACHIEVEMENTS WITH HER BURIAL IN THE PANTHEON IN PARIS.

Marie Curie was born in Warsaw, Poland in 1867. She went to Paris to study at the Sorbonne, where she met Pierre Curie, a fellow scientist and her great love.

Scientist Henri Becquerel had discovered a mysterious glow coming from uranium salts. Marie was fascinated by the glow and wanted to know what it was and why it was happening. In a stuffy shed, she and Pierre went to work. Using Pierre's electrometer, Marie examined 'glowing' compounds and discovered that the energy being produced came from the uranium atom itself. She started calling the effect 'radioactivity'. To find the source, she and Pierre ground up and filtered down other radioactive materials, in doing so discovering two new radioactive elements: polonium and radium. The Curies received a Nobel Prize in physics in 1903, for the discovery of radiation. In 1911, Marie won a Nobel Prize in chemistry for her discovery of and research into polonium and radium.

Sadly, the radiation from their experiments was making Pierre and Marie sick. Their long-term exposure made them both tired and achy – we now understand that the effects of radiation poisoning are deadly. In 1906, Pierre was killed in a horse-carriage accident. Despite her grief, Marie continued to work and discovered that radium could treat cancer. She spent hours collecting radon for hospitals even though it left her feeling weak.

France was invaded during the First World War. With her daughter, Marie created a unit of X-ray trucks, which they drove on to battlefields to help wounded soldiers.

Marie Curie did scientific work because she loved it, and dangerous work because the world needed it. Her life and achievements continue to inspire scientists today.

ONLY PERSON TO WIN A NOBEL IN TWO DIFFERENT DISCIPLINES.

COINED THE WORD 'RADIOACTIVITY'.

ALL OF HER RESEARCH IS KEPT IN LEAD-LINED CASES. THE MATERIALS ARE STILL RADIOACTIVE.

KEPT VIALS OF GLOWING RADIUM IN HER POCKETS, A DANGEROUS PRACTICE.

INHERITED PIERRE'S CHAIR AT THE SORBONNE, BECOMING THEIR FIRST FEMALE PROFESSOR.

SUFFRAGIST WHO FOUGHT FOR WOMEN'S RIGHT TO VOTE.

WORLD'S GREATEST AGROSTOLOGIST (EXPERT IN GRASS).

IDENTIFIED THOUSANDS OF TYPES OF GRASS ALL OVER THE WORLD.

'GRASS MADE IT POSSIBLE FOR THE HUMAN RACE TO ABANDON CAVE LIFE AND FOLLOW HERDS.' – MARY AGNES CHASE

MARY AGNES CHASE

BOTANIST AND SUFFRAGIST

Mary Agnes Chase was born in 1869 and grew up in Chicago, USA. She enjoyed learning about botany, sketching plants and using her savings to take botany classes at the University of Chicago and the Lewis Institute. She also worked with botanist Reverend Ellsworth Jerome Hill; he mentored Mary, and in exchange she illustrated plants for his papers.

Her impressive sketchbooks got her a job at the Chicago Field Museum, where she was a scientific illustrator for museum publications. Mary figured out how to use a microscope and do technical drawings. With her new skills, she became an illustrator for the US Department of Agriculture (USDA) in 1903.

At the USDA Mary worked as assistant to the botanist Albert Hitchcock. They collected and classified grasses in America until his death in 1935, when she became the senior botanist. Mary discovered thousands of new species of grasses from around the world and authored many books. Mary figured out which grasses were best to feed livestock. With Albert Hitchcock, she also studied commercially developed grass strains to make sure that they were as advertised. A lot of today's food has been influenced by Mary's important research.

Mary also protested for women's right to vote in the United States, even when the USDA threatened to fire her. She bravely participated in the 1918 hunger strike, in which she was jailed and force-fed. Her sacrifices helped gain women the right to vote in 1920.

Mary worked for the USDA until she retired in 1939, but was an honorary curator for the Smithsonian Institution up until her death in 1963. Her research was left to the Smithsonian, where it continues to be used.

WORKED ODD JOBS IN STOCKYARDS, A GROCERY SHOP AND A MAGAZINE.

WROTE & ILLUSTRATED A FIRST BOOK OF GRASSES THE STRUCTURE OF GRASSES EXPLAINED FOR BEGINNERS.

GIVEN AN HONORARY DEGREE FROM THE UNIVERSITY OF ILLINOIS.

WAS AN ACTIVE MEMBER IN THE NAACP.

WAS AN HONORARY FELLOW AT THE SMITHSONIAN INSTITUTION AND FELLOW AT THE LINNEAN SOCIETY OF LONDON.

HER HOME IN WASHINGTON, D.C. CALLED CASA CONTENTA BECAME A PLACE FOR LATIN AMERICAN WOMEN BOTANISTS TO STAY WHILE LEARNING IN THE US.

COLLECTED OVER 10,000 DIFFERENT TYPES OF GRASS SPECIMENS FROM AROUND THE WORLD.

TIMELINE

Throughout history, obstacles have stood in the way of women pursuing science. A lack of access to higher education and unfair wages are just two of those barriers. Let's celebrate the accomplishments women have made in education and science!

1780s

Caroline Herschel, astronomer, was the first woman to become an honorary member of the Royal Society.

1833

Oberlin College was the first college in America to admit women.

1903

Marie Curie was the first woman to receive a Nobel Prize.

1947

Marie Daly became the first African-American woman to earn a PhD in chemistry.

1955-72

The Space Race between the United States and the USSR caused a boom of innovation and engineering opportunities for women and men.

1963

Valentina Tereshkova was the first woman in space.

400 CE

Hypatia of Alexandria was the first recorded female mathematician.

1678

Elena Piscopia was the first woman in the world to receive a doctoral degree.

1715

Sybilla Masters was the first woman in the United States to get a patent for an invention, which cleaned and processed corn.

1918

Many women gained the right to vote in the United Kingdom.

1939-45

The Second World War created a workforce of women while men were at war. Female scientists were given new opportunities to show off their talents.

1946

An all-female team programmed the first all-electronic computer with the Electronic Numerical Integrator And Computer (ENIAC) project.

1964

The Equal Pay Act passed in the UK and stipulated that men and women should be paid equally for equal work. The law helps women overcome the wage gap.

1970

The Civil Rights Act made many forms of discrimination illegal in the US, ending racial segregation and giving more opportunities to African-Americans.

NOW

More women than ever before are working hard to invent, discover and explore the unknown.

DISCOVERED AND EXPLAINED THE WORKINGS OF NUCLEAR FISSION.

DISCOVERED THE ELEMENT PROTACTINIUM WITH HER LAB PARTNER OTTO HAHN.

SHOULD HAVE RECEIVED A NOBEL PRIZE.

'LIFE NEED NOT BE EASY, PROVIDED ONLY IT WAS NOT EMPTY.' —LISE MEITNER

LISE MEITNER

PHYSICIST

SHE KNEW ALBERT EINSTEIN.

HELPED AUSTRIA IN WWI AS AN X-RAY NURSE.

ENERGY FROM THE FISSION EXPERIMENT WAS DESCRIBED AS 20 MILLION TIMES MORE POWERFUL THAN TNT.

Lise Meitner was born in Vienna, Austria in 1878. She loved science but knew that, as a girl, she would need to fight to pursue her education.

After Lise received her PhD, she went to work at the Chemistry Institute in Berlin in 1907. There she met Otto Hahn, her collaborator throughout her career. Being a woman, she was unpaid and was not allowed to use the labs or even the toilets. Until the government permitted women to attend university, she did all of her radiochemistry research in a dank basement.

Lise and Otto were trying to artificially create new elements by smashing neutrons against uranium. They didn't know it yet, but they were on the brink of a discovery. Lise's research was interrupted by the Nazis' rise to power. Because she was Jewish, Lise needed to escape. In 1938, with a heavy heart, she fled to Sweden and Otto continued their work in Germany.

She and Otto secretly wrote letters about their research. He struggled to understand the results of their experiments. Lise realised that they were not creating a new element, but causing the nucleus of one atom to stretch apart and release energy. From afar, Lise discovered nuclear fission – the reaction that releases nuclear energy.

Lise was unable to return to Germany and Otto was awarded the 1944 Nobel Prize for their work – without her. Although Lise did not win the Nobel Prize, her brilliant mind changed physics forever.

109
Mt

HAD AN ELEMENT, MEITNERIUM, NAMED IN HER HONOUR.

COMPARED NUCLEAR FISSION TO THE STRETCHING OF PIZZA DOUGH.

ESCAPED FROM GERMANY WITH THE HELP OF PHYSICIST NIELS BOHR.

DINED WITH PRESIDENT TRUMAN AS THE WOMAN OF THE YEAR.

PIONEER IN ERGONOMICS, TIME AND MOTION STUDIES, AND ORGANISATIONAL PSYCHOLOGY.

FIRST WOMAN IN THE AMERICAN SOCIETY OF MECHANICAL ENGINEERS.

REINVENTED THE MODERN KITCHEN SPACE.

'WE CONSIDERED OUR TIME TOO VALUABLE TO BE DEVOTED TO ACTUAL LABOR IN THE HOME. WE WERE EXECUTIVES.' —LILLIAN GILBRETH TALKING TO A GROUP OF BUSINESS WOMEN

LILLIAN GILBRETH

PSYCHOLOGIST and INDUSTRIAL ENGINEER

Lillian Gilbreth was born in 1878 into a big family of nine children. She graduated from the University of California, Berkeley, with a master's in literature.

She met Frank Gilbreth in the middle of completing her PhD at Brown University. She was intrigued by his obsession with workplace efficiency and switched from literature to psychology. Her dissertation, 'The Psychology of Management', was the first study of how relationships affect us at work.

Together, Lillian and Frank ran a consultancy. They would study a simple task, such as bricklaying or carrying tools, and break the motions down to the most essential steps to make the workers' jobs quicker. They also wrote many books about motion and fatigue. Often, only Frank's name would appear on their work because publishers thought a male author would appear more authoritative – even though Lillian was the psychologist.

When Frank died in 1924, Lillian took charge of the company. Many of her clients did not want a woman telling them how to run factories, so Lillian focused on homemakers instead. Back then, it was common for women to spend all day cooking and cleaning. Lillian applied ergonomics and motion studies to make housewives' tasks easier. She created new tools and a new layout for kitchens that cut work time down from a day to only a few hours. It gave women more time to pursue exciting interests.

Lillian Gilbreth's designs are all around us. Whether it's the ergonomic layout of your desk or the 'work triangle' that determines the distance from the sink to the hob, her designs have been integrated into our daily lives.

TESTED OUT NEW EFFICIENCY TECHNIQUES ON HER 12 CHILDREN.

CALLED MOVEMENT UNITS 'THERBLIGS' (GILBRETH SPELLED BACKWARDS).

INVENTED THE FOOT PEDAL ON THE GARBAGE CAN AND SHELVES IN THE FRIDGE.

TESTED HER NEW KITCHEN SYSTEM BY MAKING STRAWBERRY SHORTCAKE.

USED HER KNOWLEDGE OF ERGONOMICS TO HELP DISABLED MEN AND WOMEN FIND WORK.

RECEIVED MANY HONORARY DEGREES.

NICKNAMED THE 'FIRST LADY OF MANAGEMENT'.

CREATED THE FIELD OF ABSTRACT ALGEBRA.

$$J = \sum_{i=1}^{3} \frac{\partial L}{\partial \dot{x}_i} Q[x_i] - f$$

$$= m \sum_i \dot{x}_i^2 - \left[\frac{m}{2} \sum_i \dot{x}_i^2 - V(x) \right]$$

$$= \frac{m}{2} \sum_i \dot{x}_i^2 + V(x).$$

THE NOETHER THEORY CONNECTS MATHEMATICAL SYMMETRY TO THE CONSERVATION OF ENERGY.

CONSIDERED ONE OF THE MOST IMPORTANT PEOPLE IN THE FIELD OF MATHEMATICS.

$$\left(\frac{\partial L}{\partial \dot{q}} \dot{q} - L \right) T - \frac{\partial L}{\partial \dot{q}} \frac{\partial \phi}{\partial \varepsilon}.$$

'MY METHODS ARE REALLY METHODS OF WORKING AND THINKING; THIS IS WHY THEY HAVE CREPT IN EVERYWHERE ANONYMOUSLY.'—EMMY NOETHER

EMMY NOETHER

MATHEMATICIAN AND THEORETICAL PHYSICIST

HER STUDENTS WERE CALLED 'NOETHER BOYS'.

Emmy Noether was born in Germany in 1882. She grew up in a family of mathematicians but it was against the law for women to get a higher education. She sat in the back of university classes to learn as much as she could until they finally admitted her as a student.

HER FATHER, MAX NOETHER, WAS ALSO AN IMPORTANT MATHEMATICIAN.

At the University of Erlangen, Emmy lectured unofficially without pay or job title. She made waves in the physics community with the papers she published, so around 1915, Albert Einstein recruited her to the University of Göttingen to help develop his general theory of relativity. He became a friend for life.

IF I DON'T EAT I CAN'T DO MATHEMATICS!

Emmy worked for free for seven years at Göttingen until she finally started getting paid a small amount. She developed mathematical equations that are still an important part of the way we understand physics now. She produced developments in the field of abstract algebra and made new connections between energy, time and angular momentum. In doing all of this, she developed the Noether theory.

SCHOOLS AND A MOON CRATER ARE NAMED AFTER HER.

PEOPLE WOULD MAKE FUN OF HER WEIGHT AND APPEARANCE.

Because Emmy was Jewish, the Nazi regime put her life in danger. She was fired from Göttingen for being Jewish but continued to teach from her apartment in secret. In 1933, Emmy escaped to America, where she was hired to teach at Bryn Mawr College. Unfortunately, only 18 months after she finally began receiving good pay, she became ill and died at the age of 53.

WAS A PACIFIST, DESPITE THE PERSECUTION SHE FACED IN WWII.

After her death, Albert Einstein wrote to the *New York Times* that 'Fraulein Noether was the most significant mathematical genius thus far produced since the higher education of women began.'

HER ASHES WERE BURIED AT BRYN MAWR.

CREATED SOME OF THE FIRST 'SOFTWARE' FOR ELECTRICAL ENGINEERING.

INVENTED A GRAPHICAL CALCULATOR TO HELP SOLVE EQUATIONS INVOLVING HYPERBOLIC FUNCTIONS.

EXPERT IN EQUIVALENT CIRCUITS AND GRAPHICAL ANALYSIS.

FIRST FEMALE ELECTRICAL ENGINEER.

'THERE IS NO DEMAND FOR WOMEN ENGINEERS, AS SUCH, AS THERE ARE FOR WOMEN DOCTORS, BUT THERE'S ALWAYS A DEMAND FOR ANYONE WHO CAN DO A GOOD PIECE OF WORK.' –EDITH CLARKE

EDITH CLARKE

ELECTRICAL ENGINEER

Edith Clarke was born in Maryland, USA in 1883. Tragedy struck when both of her parents died before she turned 12. She used her inheritance to pay for university.

After earning her bachelor's degree, Edith started work as a human computer. Before mechanical computers, scientists would rely on a group of people crunching complicated maths formulas to aid them in their work. At the time, human 'computing' was seen as women's work and engineering was seen as men's work.

Determined to finish her education, Edith left her job and enrolled at the Massachusetts Institute of Technology (MIT). In 1919, she became the first woman to graduate from MIT with a master's degree in electrical engineering. Still she could only find work crunching numbers. General Electric (GE) hired her, and while working as a calculator she invented a new graphical calculator. She filed a patent in 1921.

GE still wouldn't recognise her as an engineer, so she quit. For a year she travelled the world. Her absence must have made an impression, because when she returned in 1922, GE hired her as the first female electrical engineer. Edith created more efficient calculating methods, made it easier to manage complicated power systems and figured out how to get the most power out of transmission lines.

Edith retired from GE in 1945 and taught at the University of Texas for 10 years. Her work gained respect in the electrical engineering community, and in 1948 she became the first female fellow of the American Institute of Electrical Engineers. Edith Clarke proved that a woman can definitely do 'a man's job'.

FIRST WOMAN TO BE ALLOWED TO SHARE HER PAPER WITH THE AMERICAN INSTITUTE OF ELECTRICAL ENGINEERS.

PUBLISHED 18 TECHNICAL PAPERS IN 22 YEARS.

WON THE SOCIETY OF WOMEN ENGINEERS ACHIEVEMENT AWARD IN 1954.

INDUCTED INTO THE NATIONAL INVENTORS HALL OF FAME.

GREW UP WITH A READING AND WRITING LEARNING DISABILITY.

WROTE ONE OF THE MOST IMPORTANT BOOKS ON ELECTRICAL ENGINEERING: CIRCUIT ANALYSIS OF A-C POWER SYSTEMS.

FIRST FEMALE PROFESSOR IN HER FIELD IN THE US.

HELPED DESIGN HYDROELECTRIC DAMS.

GAVE US NEW INSIGHTS INTO THE ECOSYSTEMS OF WETLANDS.

CONSERVATIONIST, SUFFRAGIST AND ADVOCATE FOR CIVIL RIGHTS.

FOUNDED THE FRIENDS OF THE EVERGLADES.

HER WORK HELPED TO ESTABLISH EVERGLADES NATIONAL PARK.

'I'D LIKE TO HEAR LESS TALK ABOUT MEN AND WOMEN AND MORE TALK ABOUT CITIZENS.' —MARJORY STONEMAN DOUGLAS

MARJORY STONEMAN DOUGLAS

WRITER AND CONSERVATIONIST

In the 1940s, the Everglades in Florida, USA were seen as just one big swamp that needed draining. A feisty woman named Marjory Stoneman Douglas prevented their destruction.

Marjory was born in 1890 in Minneapolis. She always wanted to be a writer and got a job at the *Miami Herald* where her father also worked. Her father used his status as editor of the newspaper to talk about politics. As a result, Marjory understood how powerful words could be, and she began to use her own writing to talk about civil rights, the suffrage movement and environmental conservation.

Ernest Coe, a fellow conservationist, asked Marjory to help save the Everglades. Although the land was 'too buggy, too wet' for a picnic, she fell in love with its beauty. She discovered that the Everglades was not a swamp, but a river vital to Florida's ecosystem. She published *The Everglades: River of Grass* in 1947. Her work led to the creation of Everglades National Park.

Marjory also needed to protect the land from the US Army Corps of Engineers, whose dams and canals were disrupting the ecosystem. A proposed jetport threatened its destruction. Marjory's expert knowledge ensured a win. In 1969, she started the 'Friends of the Everglades' organisation and halted construction.

Despite being nearly blind, Mary continued to fight for the Everglades well into the 1990s. She was awarded the Presidential Medal of Freedom in 1993 and died at the age of 108 in 1998.

THE EVERGLADES IS HOME TO ALLIGATORS, MANATEES AND MANY SPECIES OF BIRDS AND FISH.

MARJORY UNDERSTOOD THAT THERE IS NO OTHER EVERGLADES IN THE WORLD.

IT IS A UNIQUE AND DELICATE ECOSYSTEM.

HER ASHES WERE SCATTERED OVER HER NATIONAL PARK.

SHEET FLOW

THE EVERGLADES' WIDE, SHALLOW WATERWAY MOVES VERY SLOWLY - A PHENOMENON CALLED SHEETFLOW.

BECAME KNOWN FOR HER FLOPPY HAT AND DARK ROUND GLASSES.

WORKED AS A RED CROSS NURSE IN EUROPE DURING WORLD WAR I.

FIRST AFRICAN-AMERICAN AND FIRST WOMAN TO GRADUATE FROM THE UNIVERSITY OF HAWAII.

INVENTED THE BALL METHOD.

HELPED TO CURE LEPROSY WITH HER CHEMICAL TREATMENT.

'MEN DOMINATED HIGHER EDUCATION IN 1915, AND ALICE BALL WAS ADMITTED AGAINST THE ODDS.' — MILES JACKSON, UNIVERSITY OF HAWAII PROFESSOR AND DEAN EMERITUS

ALICE BALL

─ CHEMIST ─

Alice Ball was born in Seattle, USA in 1892. Her grandfather was a photographer, and Alice was introduced to the wonders of chemistry in his darkroom. In 1915 she became the first African-American and the first woman to graduate from the University of Hawaii.

In the early 1900s, there was a public health emergency – leprosy, now known as Hansen's disease, was spreading. It causes numbness, skin lesions and damage to the nerves and eyes. Today we know that it isn't very contagious, but back then, police arrested the sick and isolated them in a leper colony on the Hawaiian island of Molokai.

At the time, there was only one source of relief for leprosy: the sticky oil of the chaulmoogra tree's seeds. But it was impossible to mix the oil with water to make a suitable treatment that could be injected. Aged 23, Alice developed a new way to treat the dense chaulmoogra oil. After isolating the ethyl esters in its fatty acids, she found the oil could be blended with water for injection. This treatment, which became known as the 'Ball method', helped the colony of people suffering from leprosy. No longer feared to be contagious, the sick did not need to be isolated. By 1918, patients could see their families and new patients were no longer forced into exile.

Alice died too young, in 1916 while in a lab – perhaps after accidentally inhaling chlorine gas. She is remembered for finding a cure for what seemed like a hopeless disease.

HER DAD WAS A FAMOUS LAWYER.

STARTING IN 1866 & INTO THE 20TH CENTURY, OVER 8000 PEOPLE WITH LEPROSY WERE SENT TO KALAUPAPA.

THE UNIVERSITY OF HAWAII HONOURED ALICE WITH A PLAQUE ON A CHAULMOOGRA TREE.

CO-PUBLISHED A PAPER IN JOURNAL OF THE AMERICAN CHEMICAL SOCIETY WHILE IN COLLEGE.

CHAULMOOGRA OIL CAUSED MAJOR STOMACH PAIN WHEN SWALLOWED.

FEBRUARY 29TH, EVERY FOUR YEARS, IS ALICE BALL DAY IN HAWAII.

DEVELOPED THE ONLY WORKING TREATMENT FOR LEPROSY UNTIL ANTIBIOTICS WERE DEVELOPED IN THE 1940s.

HER WORK HAS GIVEN US AN UNDERSTANDING OF CARBOHYDRATE METABOLISM.

CO-DISCOVERED THE CORI CYCLE.

WON A NOBEL PRIZE IN PHYSIOLOGY OR MEDICINE.

'AS A RESEARCHER THE UNFORGOTTEN MOMENTS OF MY LIFE ARE RARE ONES... WHEN THE VEIL OVER NATURE'S SECRETS SEEMS TO SUDDENLY LIFT...' —GERTY CORI

GERTY CORI

BIOCHEMIST

TOGETHER THE CORIS CREATED SYNTHETIC GLYCOGEN.

DEVELOPED THE FIRST SUPER COMPLICATED MOLECULE CREATED IN A TEST TUBE.

TOGETHER THE CORIS PUBLISHED 50 PAPERS IN 9 YEARS.

STUDIED ENZYMES AND HORMONES RELATED TO PROCESSING SUGAR.

Gerty Cori was born in 1896, in what is now the Czech Republic. She knew from an early age that she wanted to help people. At the University of Prague, she found her calling in biochemistry and received a doctorate in medicine. She also met Carl Cori.

Gerty and Carl fell deeply in love and became partners in life and in science. They were so inseparable that Carl refused a job if he couldn't work alongside his wife. Gerty was a powerhouse in the lab, known for her speed and attention to detail. As a team they were unstoppable, and decided to move to the USA.

Working first in New York and then Washington, Carl and Gerty solved the mystery of how cells use sugar for energy, a process now called the Cori cycle. Our bodies convert glucose into lactate (and back again) using our muscles and liver.

LIVER
GLUCOSE
LACTATE
BLOOD-STREAM
MUSCLE
GLUCOSE
LACTATE

In 1947, Gerty and Carl shared a Nobel Prize for their contributions to medicine. Soon after, Gerty developed a bone marrow disease but continued to work in the lab. When she became too weak to get around it, Carl would carry her. The only thing more important than their work was each other. Gerty died in 1957.

FIRST AMERICAN WOMAN TO WIN A NOBEL PRIZE.

THE CORIS' LABORATORY WAS THE TRAINING GROUND FOR 6 OTHER NOBEL PRIZE WINNERS.

HELPED US TO UNDERSTAND DIABETES.

DISCOVERED A NEW SPECIES, THE PENINSULA DRAGON LIZARD

CONSIDERED AN EXPERT IN HERPETOLOGY.

DESIGNED THE MOST COMPLICATED AND ADVANCED REPTILE HOUSE OF ITS TIME.

'WHY SHOULDN'T A WOMAN RUN A REPTILE HOUSE? WOMEN ARE AT WORK IN MY COUNTRY, AND THE REST OF THE WORLD, IN ALL TYPES OF WORK AND PROFESSIONS.' —JOAN PROCTER

'WHY SHOULDN'T A WOMAN RUN A REPTILE HOUSE? WOMEN ARE AT WORK IN MY COUNTRY, AND THE REST OF THE WORLD, IN ALL TYPES OF WORK AND PROFESSIONS.' —JOAN PROCTER

DESIGNED THE MOST COMPLICATED AND ADVANCED REPTILE HOUSE OF ITS TIME

CONSIDERED AN EXPERT IN HERPETOLOGY

DISCOVERED A NEW SPECIES, THE PENINSULA DRAGON LIZARD

GERTY CORI

BIOCHEMIST

Gerty Cori was born in 1896, in what is now the Czech Republic. She knew from an early age that she wanted to help people. At the University of Prague, she found her calling in biochemistry and received a doctorate in medicine. She also met Carl Cori.

Gerty and Carl fell deeply in love and became partners in life and in science. They were so inseparable that Carl refused a job if he couldn't work alongside his wife. Gerty was a powerhouse in the lab, known for her speed and attention to detail.

As a team they were unstoppable, and decided to move to the USA. Working first in New York and then Washington, Carl and Gerty solved the mystery of how cells use sugar for energy, a process now called the Cori cycle. Our bodies convert glucose into lactate (and back again) using our muscles and liver.

In 1947, Gerty and Carl shared a Nobel Prize for their contributions to medicine. Soon after, Gerty developed a bone marrow disease but continued to work in the lab. When she became too weak to get around it, Carl would carry her. The only thing more important than their work was each other. Gerty died in 1957.

LIVER
GLUCOSE
BLOOD-STREAM
LACTATE
MUSCLE
GLUCOSE ← LACTATE

TOGETHER THE CORIS CREATED SYNTHETIC GLYCOGEN.

DEVELOPED THE FIRST SUPER COMPLICATED MOLECULE CREATED IN A TEST TUBE.

TOGETHER THE CORIS PUBLISHED 50 PAPERS IN 9 YEARS.

STUDIED ENZYMES AND HORMONES RELATED TO PROCESSING SUGAR.

HELPED US TO UNDERSTAND DIABETES.

THE CORIS' LABORATORY WAS THE TRAINING GROUND FOR 6 OTHER NOBEL PRIZE WINNERS.

FIRST AMERICAN WOMAN TO WIN A NOBEL PRIZE.

BARBARA MCCLINTOCK

CYTOGENETICIST

Barbara McClintock was born in 1902 in Connecticut, USA and grew up in New York City. Against her mother's wishes, but with her father's support, she got a PhD in botany from Cornell University.

In 1936, she started working in genetics at the University of Missouri. She was spunky, direct and much more intelligent than many of her male peers – which made them nervous. The dean threatened to fire her if she ever got married or if her male research partner left the university. Barbara soon left to find her dream job.

She got down to business at a research facility in Cold Spring Harbor. Barbara knew that corn was a perfect tool to explore genetics – she was fascinated by corn kernels of different colours growing on the same plant. She planted a field of corn and spent hours gazing at corn cells under a microscope. She discovered that different coloured kernels have all the same genes, but in a different order. This meant that a gene could 'jump' to a different part of a chromosome and turn on and off. The discovery explained how animals, people and plants evolve to react to their environment.

Excited by her discovery, Barbara gave a lecture in 1951, but no one believed her. She didn't mind, because, as she said, 'When you know you're right, you don't care.' Over 30 years later, she finally received the recognition due to her when she was awarded a Nobel Prize.

AT THE UNIVERSITY OF MISSOURI SHE WAS CONSIDERED A TROUBLEMAKER FOR ALWAYS WEARING TROUSERS AND WORKING LATE WITH STUDENTS.

FIRST PERSON TO MAKE A COMPLETE GENETIC MAP OF CORN.

HER TECHNIQUES WERE SO ADVANCED THAT HER WORK WAS TOO CONFUSING FOR MOST SCIENTISTS AT THE TIME.

GSA

GENETICS SOCIETY OF AMERICA'S FIRST WOMAN PRESIDENT.

WAS ELECTED TO THE NATIONAL ACADEMY OF SCIENCES.

WON THE NOBEL PRIZE IN PHYSICS.

PROVED THE NUCLEAR SHELL MODEL FOR ATOMS.

GAVE US A BETTER UNDERSTANDING OF ISOTOPES.

'WHEN YOU LOVE SCIENCE, ALL YOU REALLY WANT IS TO KEEP WORKING.' —MARIA GOEPPERT-MAYER.

MARIA GOEPPERT-MAYER
THEORETICAL PHYSICIST

Maria Goeppert-Mayer solved one of the great mysteries of the universe. Born in Germany in 1906, she became one of the superstars at the University of Göttingen.

When her husband received a teaching job at Johns Hopkins University in the USA, Maria assumed it would be easy for her to get a job. But Johns Hopkins would not hire the wives of their professors. She set up a lab in a dusty attic. Maria published 10 papers on physics, quantum mechanics and chemistry, and co-wrote the textbook *Statistical Mechanics.* For nine years, she worked without pay.

Her perseverance paid off. During the Second World War, the US government noticed Maria's skills. She led a small team enriching uranium as part of America's atomic bomb research. After the war, she started her work on isotopes while teaching at Chicago University.

Isotopes happen when the number of neutrons in an atom changes. Some decay quickly; others almost never do. No one knew what made stable isotopes different, only that it had something to do with the 'magic' number of neutrons or protons they had. Maria realised that neutrons and protons rotated in orbit at different levels. The magic numbers are stable because it is easier for those amounts of protons and neutrons to spin around. Her diagrams looked like the layers of an onion.

Her nuclear shell model explained how isotopes behave. In 1960, Maria was finally given a full-time, paid job as a professor at the University of California. Soon after, she was awarded the Nobel Prize in physics.

2, 8, 20, 28, 50, 82 AND 126 ARE THE 'MAGIC NUMBERS' FOR STABLE ISOTOPES.

LEARNED NUCLEAR PHYSICS ON THE JOB IN CHICAGO.

SHE THOUGHT THE ISOTOPE MYSTERY WAS LIKE A JIGSAW PUZZLE.

SHE WAS THE SEVENTH GENERATION OF HER FAMILY TO BECOME A PROFESSOR.

HER NICKNAME WAS ONION MADONNA.

WAS A HEAVY SMOKER, OFTEN SMOKING TWO CIGARETTES AT ONCE, WHICH CAUSED SERIOUS HEALTH PROBLEMS LATER IN LIFE.

INVENTED THE FIRST COMPILER, FOREVER CHANGING HOW WE USE COMPUTERS.

CREATED COBOL, THE FIRST COMPLEX COMPUTER LANGUAGE.

PIONEERED THE STANDARDS FOR TESTING COMPUTER SYSTEMS.

'PEOPLE ARE ALLERGIC TO CHANGE. YOU HAVE TO GET OUT AND SELL THE IDEA.' —GRACE HOPPER—

GRACE HOPPER

NAVY ADMIRAL AND COMPUTER SCIENTIST

Grace Hopper was a relentless trailblazer, recognised as the mother of computer programming. She was born in New York City in 1906, and earned a PhD in mathematics from Yale in 1934. Grace was working as a maths professor when the United States entered the Second World War. In 1943, Grace quit her job to join the Women Accepted for Volunteer Emergency Service.

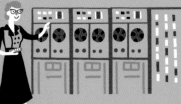

The Navy sent her to Harvard to program one of the first-ever electronic computers. Back then, calculations were done by a large group of people. The new Mark I would be able to solve equations that were too complicated for that old system. Grace's team used the Mark I to solve important problems for the war effort, including the implosion equation for the Manhattan Project.

After the war, Grace joined the private sector. At the time, programmers needed an advanced degree in maths and used binary code to program. Grace Hopper thought it would be easier to just 'talk' to a computer in English. Everyone thought Grace was nuts, but she proved them wrong when she invented the first compiler. It led her to create COBOL, the first universal computer language. Thanks to Grace, anyone can learn to code!

Grace returned to the Navy in 1967. Even after she retired, just short of turning 80, she continued to lecture and teach – always reminding the world that the most damaging phrase in the English language is 'we've always done it this way'.

RECEIVED THE DEFENSE DISTINGUISHED SERVICE MEDAL.

HAD A BACKWARD CLOCK IN HER OFFICE TO REMIND HER THAT THINGS DON'T HAVE TO WORK JUST ONE WAY.

APPEARED ON THE LATE SHOW WITH DAVID LETTERMAN AND 60 MINUTES.

COINED THE TERM 'DEBUGGING' WHEN A MOTH GOT CAUGHT IN THE COMPUTER.

HER GREAT-GRANDFATHER WAS ALSO IN THE NAVY.

THE MARK I COMPUTER WAS 15 METRES WIDE.

HAD A JOLLY ROGER PIRATE FLAG ON HER DESK BECAUSE SHE WAS RELENTLESS IN GETTING WHAT HER TEAM NEEDED.

← 30 CENTIMETRES →

FAMOUS FOR HER CUT WIRES SHOWING THE DISTANCE THAT ELECTRICITY TRAVELS IN A NANOSECOND.

TAUGHT THE WORLD ABOUT THE OCEAN'S ECOSYSTEMS.

INSPIRED THE US ENVIRONMENTAL PROTECTION AGENCY.

WROTE AWARD-WINNING BOOKS: THE SEA AROUND US, THE EDGE OF THE SEA, UNDER THE SEA WIND & SILENT SPRING.

'THE HUMAN RACE IS CHALLENGED MORE THAN EVER BEFORE TO DEMONSTRATE OUR MASTERY, NOT OVER NATURE BUT OF OURSELVES.' – RACHEL CARSON

RACHEL CARSON

MARINE BIOLOGIST, CONSERVATIONIST <u>AND</u> AUTHOR

From an early age, Rachel Carson could be found looking at birds, bugs and fish. She was born in 1907 and grew up on a farm in Pennsylvania, USA. She got her master's in zoology at Johns Hopkins University then worked at the Bureau of Fisheries, writing radio scripts about fish. When she wasn't at her job, she wrote about wildlife.

Rachel's first book, *Under the Sea Wind*, got little attention, but her next book, *The Sea Around Us*, became a sensation. She won the National Book Award and quit her job to write *The Edge of the Sea*.

In the 1950s, the US government and private industry started to overuse the pesticide DDT. We now know that DDT is highly toxic and can cause liver damage and seizures. DDT was being used everywhere, from insect repellent to crop spray – but it killed more than just pests.

Rachel received a letter from an old friend saying that a plane spraying DDT had killed all the song birds in her sanctuary. This inspired Rachel to write her greatest book, *Silent Spring*. Rachel's research found that DDT was poisoning livestock, killing fish and fatally weakening birds' eggs.

Chemical companies slandered her work, but Rachel would not be bullied. The truth about DDT became public – Rachel even spoke in front of the US Senate. She wrote *Silent Spring* while battling cancer, and she died two years after it was published. Her work led to the creation of the US Environmental Protection Agency and inspired the global environmental movement.

WROTE A BOOK ABOUT BIRDS WHEN SHE WAS EIGHT.

WAS PUBLISHED IN A CHILDREN'S MAGAZINE WHEN SHE WAS 11.

THE NATIONAL ENVIRONMENTAL POLICY ACT (NEPA) WAS PASSED IN RESPONSE TO SILENT SPRING.

CHEMICAL COMPANIES SPENT NEARLY $250,000 ON A SMEAR CAMPAIGN TO DISCREDIT RACHEL.

HER GOVERNMENT RADIO PROGRAMME ABOUT FISH WAS CALLED 'ROMANCE UNDER THE WATERS'.

SILENT SPRING WAS EXHAUSTIVELY RESEARCHED: IT HAS A 55-PAGE BIBLIOGRAPHY.

AWARDED THE PRESIDENTIAL MEDAL OF FREEDOM IN 1980.

LAB TOOLS

Problem-solving requires testing and experimentation, and having the right equipment can make or break research. These women did their work anywhere they could – from dusty attics and tiny sheds to state-of-the-art labs.

WELL PLATE →

TEST TUBES

RUBBER STOPPERS →

EYE → DROPPER

TEST TUBE HOLDER ←

SCOOPULA →

CRUCIBLE & COVER

IRON RING ←

MICROSCOPE

UTILITY CLAMP →

MAGNET →

PIPETTE

THERMOMETER

ROUND-BOTTOM FLASK

WIRE BRUSH ←

MICRO PIPETTE

SEPARATING FUNNEL →

TWO-NECK ROUND-BOTTOM FLASK

SPATULA →

PLUNGER ←

TEST TUBE RACK

BÜCHNER FUNNEL

CORK STOPPERS

PETRI DISH

SLIDE

BÜCHNER FLASK

WATCH GLASS

TONGS

RULER

LAB BURNER

SAFETY GOGGLES

WIRE GAUZE

BURETTE

WASH BOTTLE

FLORENCE FLASK

SCALPEL

FUNNEL

MAGNIFYING GLASS

EVAPORATING DISH

GRADUATED CYLINDER

LIGHTER

PIPE-STEM TRIANGLE

24-WELL PLATE

POWDER FUNNEL

BUNSEN BURNER

FORCEPS

FILE

PESTLE & MORTAR

EXTENSION CLAMP

CONICAL FLASK

BEAKER

AWARDED THE NOBEL PRIZE IN PHYSIOLOGY OR MEDICINE.

DISCOVERED THE NERVE GROWTH FACTOR.

WAS AN ITALIAN SENATOR FOR LIFE.

'ABOVE ALL, DON'T FEAR DIFFICULT MOMENTS. THE BEST COMES FROM THEM.' —RITA LEVI-MONTALCINI

RITA LEVI-MONTALCINI

NEUROLOGIST AND ITALIAN SENATOR

Rita Levi-Montalcini was born in 1909 in Italy to a rich Jewish family. Her father expected her to become a proper lady and marry well, but she hated finishing school and was determined to become a doctor.

Though Rita graduated summa cum laude from medical school in 1936, she had no real job prospects. Italy was one of the Axis powers in the Second World War, and in 1938, anti-Semitic laws forbade Jewish people to practise medicine. But nothing could keep Rita from pursuing her dreams. She created a makeshift lab in her bedroom, borrowing eggs from farmers and using sewing needles to dissect the nervous systems of embryonic chicks. She wanted to know why and how nerve cells developed. By severing the limbs of the chick embryo, she documented how the motor neurons began to grow and then die. This work laid the foundation for her entire career.

After the Second World War, Rita re-entered the formal scientific world at Washington University in Missouri, USA. While learning how to grow tissues in a glass dish, Rita observed that a tumour sample was making the nerve cells in the same dish grow very quickly. By experimenting with snake venom, tumours and mouse saliva, she discovered nerve growth factor, a protein that regulates nerve growth and keeps our neurons healthy. This was a very important finding for understanding and fighting diseases.

Rita received the 1986 Nobel Prize in physiology or medicine. She went on to become a senator-for-life in the Italian government, where she fought for civic equality and promoted the sciences.

SHE WAS APPOINTED TO THE PONTIFICAL ACADEMY OF SCIENCES BY POPE PAUL VI —

AND SHOOK THE POPE'S HAND INSTEAD OF KISSING IT.

SNUCK LAB MICE ON TO A PLANE FOR HER RESEARCH.

WORKED UNTIL SHE DIED AT AGE 103.

ONCE LECTURED IN A PRESSED NIGHT GOWN WHEN HER LUGGAGE WAS LOST.

SHE DID IMPORTANT RESEARCH ON HUMAN MAST CELLS AND THEIR RELATION TO NGF.

SHARED THE NOBEL PRIZE WITH HER LAB PARTNER AND COLLABORATOR STANLEY COHEN.

DISCOVERED THE STRUCTURE OF PENICILLIN, VITAMIN B12 AND INSULIN.

SHE INVENTED TECHNIQUES TO USE X-RAY CRYSTALLOGRAPHY TO MAP COMPLEX MOLECULES.

WON A NOBEL PRIZE IN CHEMISTRY AND THE ORDER OF MERIT.

'I WAS CAPTURED FOR LIFE BY CHEMISTRY AND BY CRYSTALS.' — DOROTHY HODGKIN

DOROTHY HODGKIN

BIOCHEMIST AND X-RAY CRYSTALLOGRAPHER

Born in 1910, Dorothy Hodgkin grew up in Britain but visited her parents on archaeological sites in Sudan, gaining early fieldwork experience. Aged 13, she found a mystery mineral and determined it was ilmenite crystal.

Dorothy quickly developed a love of crystallography, the study of atomic and molecular structure. It could take months or even years of observation, combined with complicated maths, to understand molecular structure. Dorothy was accepted into Oxford University to study it when there was a strict cap on women's admission. In 1934, she began to research and teach – in a dark, dusty basement, surrounded by electrical wires and skeleton specimens. She impressed everyone when she mapped the structure of cholesterol, and she became the go-to person for mapping seemingly unsolvable molecules.

Dorothy set out to discover the structure of the antibiotic penicillin. Chemists needed this information to create large synthetic batches of the medicine. In 1945, after four years of hard work, she cracked the code. She helped save millions of lives with this discovery.

Dorothy continued to do pioneering work. While working on the vitamin B12's structure, she teamed up with students to create a computer program that could map structures more quickly. She won a Nobel Prize for chemistry in 1964, for her work uncovering the structures of important biochemical substances, including B12. Dorothy also mapped the structure of insulin, which helped create medication for diabetics.

In her old age, Dorothy travelled the world giving lectures. She spoke about diabetes awareness and campaigned for world peace until her death in 1994.

CHEMISTRY CLASS WAS BOYS-ONLY IN SECONDARY SCHOOL—

SHE GOT SPECIAL PERMISSION TO BE IN CLASS.

SHE WAS NICKNAMED THE 'GENTLE GENIUS' AND THE 'CLEVEREST WOMAN IN ENGLAND'.

WON MANY AWARDS, INCLUDING THE LENIN PEACE PRIZE.

SHE HELPED TO START THE INTERNATIONAL UNION OF CRYSTALLOGRAPHY.

SHE WAS FRIENDS WITH MARGARET THATCHER.

A FELLOW SCIENTIST BET THAT IF SHE FOUND THE STRUCTURE OF PENICILLIN, HE WOULD QUIT & BECOME A MUSHROOM FARMER (HE DIDN'T).

DISPROVED A 'LAW
OF CONSERVATION
OF PARITY'.

AWARDED THE MEDAL OF SCIENCE.

HELPED DEVELOP THE FUEL
FOR THE ATOMIC BOMB.

'THE MAIN STUMBLING BLOCK IN THE WAY OF ANY PROGRESS IS AND ALWAYS HAS BEEN
UNIMPEACHABLE TRADITION.' — CHIEN-SHIUNG WU

CHIEN-SHIUNG WU

EXPERIMENTAL PHYSICIST

Chien-Shiung Wu was born in China in 1912, when not all women were expected to become educated. Luckily, her father was a pioneer for women's rights and started the first school in their town for girls. In 1936, Chien-Shiung headed to the US to study experimental physics.

After graduating with a PhD from the University of California in 1940, Chien-Shiung became a professor at Princeton University and Smith College. She was known to be demanding but pushed her students to be their best, and they loved her for it.

The Second World War was fought and won with science, and in 1944 Chien-Shiung was recruited to work on the Manhattan Project. She helped develop a way to enrich uranium into the isotopes needed to fuel the atomic bomb, and to develop radiation detectors for the project.

After the war, Chien-Shiung started her work on beta decay at Columbia University. A theory called 'the law of conservation of parity' predicted that radioactive atoms would decay in a symmetrical way. But a new particle was discovered that didn't follow the rules. No one actually observed this wonky particle until Chien-Shiung did. With determination and a very strong magnet, Chien-Shiung observed that the electrons of these atoms broke away asymmetrically, disproving the law of conservation of parity.

She published a book, *Beta Decay*, and was given many awards and honours. She researched and lectured into her old age.

WON THE 1975 NATIONAL MEDAL OF SCIENCE.

WHILE BEING INTERVIEWED FOR THE TOP-SECRET MANHATTAN PROJECT, SHE ALREADY KNEW WHAT THEY WERE WORKING ON JUST BY LOOKING AT AN EQUATION LEFT ON A BLACKBOARD.

HOMEWORK

NICKNAMED 'FIRST LADY OF PHYSICS'.

RESEARCHED SICKLE-CELL DISEASE.

APS

FIRST WOMAN ELECTED A FELLOW TO THE AMERICAN PHYSICAL SOCIETY.

HER NAME TRANSLATES AS 'COURAGEOUS HERO'.

IS IN THE NATIONAL INVENTORS HALL OF FAME.

HER WORK IS USED FOR CONTROLLING TORPEDOES, WI-FI, BLUETOOTH & MILITARY COMMUNICATION.

CO-INVENTED THE TECHNOLOGY TO USE FREQUENCY-HOPPING SPREAD SPECTRUM COMMUNICATION.

'[MY FATHER] MADE ME UNDERSTAND THAT I MUST MAKE MY OWN DECISIONS, MOLD MY OWN CHARACTER, THINK MY OWN THOUGHTS.' — HEDY LAMARR

HEDY LAMARR

INVENTOR and FILM ACTRESS

You may already know that Hedy Lamarr was an actress during Hollywood's Golden Age – but did you know she was also a genius inventor? Hedy was born Hedwig Eva Maria Kiesler in 1914 in Austria. She dreamed of being an actress – and made it a reality. When her controlling husband wanted to end her acting career, she left him. Soon a film producer gave her an acting contract and a new name.

Hedy also had a secret workshop where she tinkered with inventions. During the Second World War, Hedy identified a problem she thought she could fix: the US Navy's radio-guided torpedoes were easy to signal-jam, which caused them to go off course.

At a dinner party, she met composer George Antheil. Together they realised that a radio signal could change frequencies with the same technology a piano player uses to change notes, making the signal impossible to jam. Working together, they developed the frequency-hopping spread spectrum (FHSS). Hedy received a patent in 1942, but the US military shelved her idea. It wasn't until the Cuban missile crisis in 1962 that they realised FHSS was a goldmine. Hedy's technology was used to control torpedoes and communication – especially between multiple electronic devices. FHSS is now the foundation for the GPS, Wi-Fi and Bluetooth technologies we use every day.

The patent had expired by the time FHSS was in use, but Hedy won many awards. She was inducted into the National Inventors Hall of Fame in 2014, 14 years after her death.

TINKERED WITH A NEW TRAFFIC LIGHT AND A BETTER TISSUE BOX.

RECEIVED THE ELECTRONIC FRONTIER FOUNDATION PIONEER AWARD IN 1997.

STARRED IN FILMS WITH CLARK GABLE, SPENCER TRACY AND JIMMY STEWART.

HOWARD HUGHES LENT HER CHEMISTS TO HELP HER CREATE A NEW TABLET TO CARBONATE WATER. (IT WAS UNSUCCESSFUL).

HAS A STAR IN THE HOLLYWOOD WALK OF FAME.

EX-HUSBAND, FRITZ MANDL, WAS A WEAPONS MANUFACTURER.

HEDY LEARNED TRADE SECRETS FROM OVERHEARING HIS DINNER CONVERSATIONS.

HER WORK WON THE SUPREME COURT CASE BROWN V. BOARD OF EDUCATION.

CO-FOUNDED THE NORTHSIDE CENTER FOR CHILD DEVELOPMENT IN HARLEM, NEW YORK CITY.

HER DOLL TEST AND COLOURING TEST PROVED THAT SEGREGATION HURTS CHILDREN.

'WHAT DID IT MEAN THAT ALL THESE CHILDREN WERE IN ONE PLACE?... THEY'RE ISOLATED FROM WHITES, AND THEY CAN NEVER LEARN THAT THEY'RE JUST AS GOOD AS WHITES ... YOU HAVE TO GET THESE CHILDREN DESEGREGATED.' –MAMIE PHIPPS CLARK

MAMIE PHIPPS CLARK

PSYCHOLOGIST AND CIVIL RIGHTS ACTIVIST

Slavery in America was abolished in 1865, but African-Americans did not gain full equality until the Fair Housing Act of 1968. For over 100 years, black Americans were denied the right to vote, to a proper education and to exist in certain places.

Mamie Phipps Clark was born in 1917 in Arkansas. Racial segregation meant that Mamie was not allowed in shops owned by white people and had to attend poorly funded black-only schools.

Mamie met her husband and future partner in psychology, Kenneth Clark, at Howard University. At Howard, Mamie's master's thesis showed that race is an integral part of a child's identity. She realised she could use psychology to prove that segregation was wrong.

KENNETH CLARK

Together the Clarks started the Doll Experiment, travelling the country and comparing the responses of children in segregated and integrated schools. They gave children identical black and white dolls and asked, 'Which doll do you want to play with? Is this doll pretty? Is this doll nice?' Black children identified with the black doll, but if they were in segregated schools they said the black doll was ugly and bad – and that they themselves were also bad. Mamie and Kenneth had proof that segregation damaged children and caused self-hate. This study was used in the 1954 Supreme Court case *Brown v. Board of Education*, which ended segregation in public schools.

The effects of segregation are still felt in America. The wound will need pioneers like Mamie to fully heal.

SHE GRADUATED MAGNA CUM LAUDE FROM HOWARD UNIVERSITY.

CHOSE HER CAREER BECAUSE SHE ALWAYS WANTED TO WORK WITH CHILDREN.

WORKED AS A COUNSELLOR FOR HOMELESS AFRICAN-AMERICAN GIRLS AT THE RIVERDALE HOME IN NEW YORK.

THE COLOURING TEST ALSO PROVED THAT SEGREGATION WARPS SELF-WORTH.

WAS THE SECOND AFRICAN-AMERICAN (HER HUSBAND WAS THE FIRST) TO RECEIVE A PH.D FROM COLUMBIA UNIVERSITY.

WAS THE DIRECTOR OF NORTHSIDE CENTER FOR CHILD DEVELOPMENT FROM 1946 UNTIL SHE RETIRED IN 1979.

EQUAL RIGHTS

EQUAL RIGHTS

HAS SAVED THOUSANDS OF LIVES WITH THE DRUGS SHE DEVELOPED.

HELPED TO DEVELOP DRUGS TO FIGHT CANCER, AIDS, HERPES AND MANY MORE DISEASES.

FIRST WOMAN INDUCTED INTO THE NATIONAL INVENTORS HALL OF FAME.

'DON'T LET OTHERS DISCOURAGE YOU OR TELL YOU THAT YOU CAN'T DO IT. IN MY DAY I WAS TOLD WOMEN DIDN'T GO INTO CHEMISTRY. I SAW NO REASON WHY WE COULDN'T.' —GERTRUDE ELION

GERTRUDE ELION

PHARMACOLOGIST AND BIOCHEMIST

Gertrude Elion was born in 1918 and grew up in New York City. She loved all of her subjects in high school and graduated early at age 15. When her grandfather died of cancer, she decided to dedicate her life to fighting the disease.

During the Great Depression, universities prioritised hiring men. Gertrude graduated with high honours from university, but chemistry jobs were scarce. Finally, she found a home for her cancer research at the Burroughs Wellcome pharmaceutical company.

Gertrude studied the difference between healthy and abnormal cells so they could create drugs that destroyed only unhealthy cells. She also studied the nucleic acids in DNA and how they could stop tumours from spreading. She worked towards finishing her PhD at night. Her graduate school demanded that she quit her job, but she loved her work so much that she quit the PhD programme instead. It was the right choice; Gertrude went on to create medications that saved thousands of lives. In 1950, she created two drugs to treat leukemia, which began a new era of cancer research.

Another major breakthrough came in 1978, when she created a way for antivirals to target a virus without harming healthy cells. A resulting drug is used to treat herpes and other viruses.

Gertrude's drug research saved thousands of lives and made huge advances in drug treatment. When asked her favourite achievement, she responded, 'I don't discriminate among my children'.

WON THE NOBEL PRIZE IN PHYSIOLOGY OR MEDICINE IN 1988.

SHE CREATED MEDICATION FOR GOUT AND SHINGLES.

BECAME A DEPARTMENT HEAD AT BURROUGHS WELLCOME.

AFTER RETIRING, BECAME A RESEARCH PROFESSOR AT DUKE UNIVERSITY.

HER FIRST FULL-TIME CHEMISTRY JOB WAS TESTING PICKLES FOR GROCERY SHOPS.

HER HERPES DRUG LED TO AZT, WHICH FIGHTS AIDS.

WAS PRESIDENT OF THE AMERICAN ASSOCIATION FOR CANCER RESEARCH AND PARTICIPATED IN MANY MORE CANCER ORGANISATIONS.

PHYSICIST, SPACE SCIENTIST AND NASA MATHEMATICIAN.

$$v_e = \sqrt{\frac{2GM}{r}}$$

WON THE NASA LUNAR ORBITER AWARD & THE NASA SPECIAL ACHIEVEMENT AWARD.

CALCULATED THE FLIGHT PATH FOR THE FIRST MANNED MISSION TO THE MOON.

HAS WORKED ON NASA'S MERCURY MISSIONS, SPACE SHUTTLES AND PLANS FOR THE MISSION TO MARS.

'[THE OTHER WOMEN] DIDN'T ASK QUESTIONS OR TAKE THE TASK ANY FURTHER. I ASKED QUESTIONS; I WANTED TO KNOW WHY. THEY GOT USED TO ME ASKING QUESTIONS AND BEING THE ONLY WOMAN THERE.' —KATHERINE JOHNSON

KATHERINE JOHNSON

PHYSICIST AND MATHEMATICIAN

Katherine Johnson was born in 1918 in West Virginia, USA. She excelled in school and enrolled at West Virginia State College when she was only 15 years old.

Katherine assumed she was going to become a maths teacher or a nurse like other women she knew. But when she met her university professor, the famous mathematician W. W. Schieffelin Claytor, he inspired Katherine to become a research mathematician.

When she was 18, Katherine graduated from university. It was the height of the Great Depression and jobs were scarce, so she taught in high school. By the 1950s, NASA began to have more openings for African-American female computers. Katherine applied and got a job. She was not allowed in meetings, so she asked if it was against the law. Her boldness and curiosity paid off, and she was included.

Calculating flight paths involved complicated geometry equations, and Katherine was extremely good at these. She successfully calculated the launch window of the 1961 manned Mercury mission and quickly became a leader in calculating trajectory. She did most of the calculations on the path for the first manned mission to the Moon in 1969, and was also in charge of checking the maths of NASA's brand-new mechanical computers. The Apollo mission was a success, and her crucial contributions made it possible!

Katherine retired after 33 years of service in 1986. Her work has helped astronauts visit the stars and come safely back to Earth.

1, 2, 3...

AS A LITTLE GIRL, SHE LOVED NUMBERS AND WOULD COUNT EVERYTHING SHE COULD FIND.

IN 2015, SHE WON THE PRESIDENTIAL MEDAL OF FREEDOM AT AGE 97.

CO-AUTHORED 26 SCIENTIFIC PAPERS.

STUDIED MATHS AND FRENCH AT UNIVERSITY.

THE MOON & THE APOLLO SHUTTLE MOVE AT DIFFERENT SPEEDS — HER CALCULATIONS ENSURED THEY WOULD MEET.

WAS THE 1997 MATHEMATICIAN OF THE YEAR.

NASA

HELPED WRITE THE FIRST TEXTBOOK ABOUT SPACE TRAVEL.

RECEIVED AN HONORARY DOCTOR OF LAW DEGREE FROM THE STATE UNIVERSITY OF NEW YORK.

CO-FOUNDED THE AMERICAN SOCIETY OF CLINICAL ONCOLOGY.

HER NEW CHEMO TECHNIQUES SAVED MILLIONS OF LIVES.

DEVELOPED NEW WAYS TO TEST CHEMO DRUGS AND TO TREAT HARD-TO-REACH TUMOURS.

'NOT ONLY WAS [JANE WRIGHT'S] WORK SCIENTIFIC, BUT IT WAS VISIONARY FOR THE WHOLE SCIENCE OF ONCOLOGY.' —DR. SANDRA SWAIN, *THE NEW YORK TIMES*

JANE COOKE WRIGHT

ONCOLOGIST

Jane Cooke Wright was born into a family of doctors in 1919. Her grandfather was the first African-American to graduate from Yale's medical school, and her father founded Harlem Hospital's Cancer Research Foundation.

In the 1940s, a cancer diagnosis was often considered a death sentence. After Jane graduated from New York Medical College in 1945, she started her career in cancer research, working with her father at Harlem Hospital. When her father died, Jane became the head of the cancer research centre aged 33.

Jane developed new techniques that saved precious time. Instead of testing chemo drugs on the patient directly, Jane tested only samples of their cancer tissue. This allowed her to quickly create the most effective treatment. She understood that each person needed a unique cocktail of chemotherapy drugs. Jane also innovated a new way to treat hard-to-reach tumours. Surgically removing tumours sometimes necessitated removing whole organs, so Jane developed a less invasive way to precisely deliver chemo using a catheter.

Jane was a co-founder of the American Society of Clinical Oncology and the associate dean of the New York Medical College (ASCO). She was also the first female president of the New York Cancer Society. In a time when there were few African-American doctors, and even fewer who were women, Jane was a radical trailblazer.

SHE ALMOST BECAME A PAINTER IN COLLEGE.

DEVELOPED BETTER PROGRAMMES TO STUDY STROKE, HEART DISEASE AND CANCER.

LED DELEGATIONS OF DOCTORS IN AFRICA, CHINA AND EASTERN EUROPE.

HELPED TO TEST NEW CANCER DRUGS LIKE METHOTREXATE.

NICKNAMED 'THE MOTHER OF CHEMOTHERAPY'.

WORKED ON THE PRESIDENT'S COMMISSION ON HEART DISEASE, CANCER AND STROKE IN 1964.

DID CRITICAL WORK ON MOLECULAR STRUCTURES OF DNA, RNA, VIRUSES, COAL & GRAPHITE.

DISCOVERED THE DNA DOUBLE HELIX.

PIONEERED RESEARCH ON THE TOBACCO MOSAIC VIRUS & POLIO.

'SCIENCE AND EVERYDAY LIFE CANNOT AND SHOULD NOT BE SEPARATED.' -ROSALIND FRANKLIN

ROSALIND FRANKLIN

⬡ CHEMIST AND X-RAY CRYSTALLOGRAPHER ⬡

Rosalind Franklin was born in 1920 in London. Her father disapproved of women going to university, but she went on to earn a PhD in physical chemistry from Cambridge.

The big question of the day was 'What is the shape of DNA?' Scientists knew that DNA formed the building blocks of the body, but they had no idea what it really looked like. Rosalind Franklin was on the case at King's College.

She spent hours using an X-ray on the delicate fibres of DNA, capturing a famous photo proving DNA is a double helix. Meanwhile, two scientists, James Watson and Francis Crick, were also trying to figure out the structure of DNA. They peeked at Rosalind's work without her permission, and used her findings to publish their own work without giving her credit. Rosalind left the toxic work environment of King's College and continued her research. She went on to a top research lab and started researching the tobacco mosaic and polio viruses.

Rosalind died from cancer in 1958 at only 37; Watson and Crick won a Nobel Prize four years later. Watson wrote scathing comments about Rosalind in his book *The Double Helix*, also admitting that he had looked at her data. People started to figure out what really happened, and Rosalind is remembered as a woman who should have won a Nobel Prize. Now that we know her story, we can celebrate all that she accomplished!

BOYS ONLY

ALL OF THE DINING HALLS & PUBS AROUND KING'S COLLEGE WERE MEN-ONLY.

KNEW SHE WANTED TO BE A SCIENTIST WHEN SHE WAS 15 YEARS OLD.

PHOTO 51 PROVED THE DOUBLE HELIX STRUCTURE.

CREATED A HUGE, ACCURATE TOBACCO MOSAIC VIRUS SCULPTURE FOR THE WORLD'S FAIR.

LEARNED X-RAY CRYSTALLOGRAPHY IN FRANCE.

RESEARCHED CHARCOAL TO BE USED IN GAS MASKS DURING WWII.

DEVELOPED THE RIA TECHNIQUE TO MEASURE HORMONES IN THE BODY.

WON THE 1977 NOBEL PRIZE IN PHYSIOLOGY OR MEDICINE.

GAVE US A BETTER UNDERSTANDING OF DIABETES AND OTHER HORMONE-RELATED DISEASES.

'WE MUST BELIEVE IN OURSELVES OR NO ONE ELSE WILL BELIEVE IN US; WE MUST MATCH OUR ASPIRATIONS WITH THE COMPETENCE, COURAGE AND DETERMINATION TO SUCCEED.' —ROSALYN YALOW

ROSALYN YALOW

MEDICAL PHYSICIST

Rosalyn Yalow was always a fighter – her family told stories about her standing up to teachers when she was a child. Born in New York in 1921, she spent her youth at Yankees games and the library.

After completing her PhD at the University of Illinois in 1945, the Veterans Administration Medical Center offered Rosalyn a job figuring out ways to use radioisotopes in medicine. Without much funding, she turned a cleaning cupboard into one of America's first radioisotope labs. Her lab partner was Solomon Berson; they would become best friends.

Rosalyn and Solomon created a very sensitive way to measure hormones in the body. They tagged the hormone with a radioactive isotope and then measured the amount of antibodies that were created. Their radioimmunoassay (RIA) technique is still used today. Rosalyn and Solomon then used RIA to make discoveries about how insulin worked inside the body, illuminating the difference between type 1 and type 2 diabetes. This helped doctors medicate patients properly.

In 1972, Solomon died of a heart attack. Rosalyn was heartbroken; he had been like a brother. She knew that she would be taken less seriously now that she was a lone female scientist. She worked harder than ever, releasing over 60 research articles in only four years.

Rosalyn's hard work paid off; she was awarded many prizes and honours, including the Nobel Prize in 1977. Her research continues to save lives to this day.

UNDERSTOOD HARD WORK AND HELPED HER MUM AT THE NECKWEAR FACTORY TO AFFORD HER OWN BRACES.

INSULIN FROM PIGS AND COWS WAS BEING USED TO TREAT DIABETES – ROSALYN FIGURED OUT WHY IT DIDN'T WORK.

RIA IS USED TO SCREEN UNBORN BABIES FOR DEADLY DISEASES, DETECT THYROID PROBLEMS AND MAKE SURE BLOOD BANKS ARE SAFE.

TOTALLY WORTH IT!

SHE HUNG FROM THE RAFTERS TO HEAR PHYSICIST ENRICO FERMI SPEAK IN A PACKED LECTURE HALL.

RENAMED HER LAB 'THE SOLOMON A. BERSON RESEARCH LAB' AFTER HIS DEATH.

KEPT CHILLED CHAMPAGNE IN HER OFFICE EVERY YEAR JUST IN CASE SHE WON THE NOBEL PRIZE.

HELPED US BETTER UNDERSTAND BACTERIA & VIRUSES.

DISCOVERED LAMBDA PHAGE VIRUS.

PIONEER OF BACTERIAL GENETICS.

INVENTED REPLICA PLATING TO STUDY MUTATIONS.

'YOU CAN BEGIN ANYTIME, EVEN THOUGH IT TAKES A LIFETIME TO BE GOOD.' —ESTHER LEDERBERG

ESTHER LEDERBERG

MICROBIOLOGIST

Esther Lederberg was born into a poor family in New York City in 1922. She studied genetics at Stanford University, where she got her master's degree in 1946. That year she married Joshua Lederberg, a molecular biologist. She got her doctorate from the University of Wisconsin, where she and Joshua studied bacteria together.

SHE WAS SO POOR IN GRAD SCHOOL THAT SHE ALLEGEDLY ATE THE LEFTOVER FROG LEGS FROM HER LAB DISSECTIONS.

Esther discovered a new type of bacteriophage (a virus that infects bacteria). Rather than immediately killing its host bacteria, lamda phage hid inside the bacteria's DNA until its host was about to die; then it would spread. Studying it has given us a better understanding of RNA, DNA and diseases like tumour viruses.

FIRST TRIED REPLICA PLATING WITH HER POWDER PUFF.

WENT TO UNIVERSITY TO STUDY FRENCH LITERATURE; THEN CHANGED HER MAJOR TO BIOCHEMISTRY.

Esther also created a new way of studying mutations in bacteria called replica plating. Before this, studying mutations took a long time. She used velvet to stamp bacteria into petri dishes containing different types of chemicals; it was easy to see which mutated bacteria lived or died.

PUBLISHED HER DISCOVERY OF LAMBDA PHAGE IN MICROBIAL GENETICS BULLETIN IN 1951.

LOVED MEDIEVAL MUSIC AND FOUNDED A RECORDER ORCHESTRA.

This method allowed her team to prove that bacteria can mutate spontaneously. They also found that some bacteria were resistant to antibiotics even before having contact with them. Their work led to Joshua winning the Nobel Prize in 1958; in his award speech, he never thanked Esther for her research.

They divorced in 1966. Esther continued her work at Stanford and became the director of the Plasmid Reference Center. She loved her work so much that she continued her research even after she officially retired.

SECOND MARRIAGE WAS TO MATTHEW SIMON, AN ENGINEER WHO ALSO LOVED MEDIEVAL MUSIC.

HELPED TO PROVE THAT BACTERIA CAN SPONTANEOUSLY MUTATE.

STATISTICS IN STEM

The United States carries out a census every 10 years. The 2011 census gave the world insight into how poorly women are represented in the STEM (science, technology, engineering and maths) fields. From the mid-twentieth century to the new millennium, there has been a definite increase in female scientists, but women are still underrepresented in these fields. That simply won't do. There are girls in every country right now who could grow up to cure cancer, explore a new galaxy or discover a new type of energy.

GENDER GAP PERCENTS

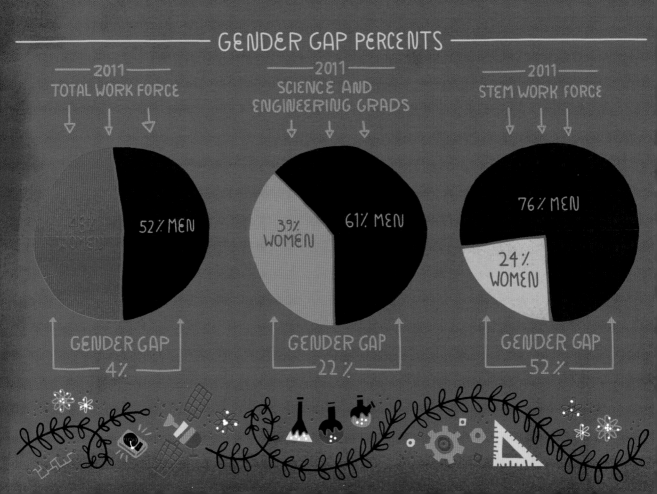

2011
TOTAL WORK FORCE

48% WOMEN
52% MEN

GENDER GAP 4%

2011
SCIENCE AND ENGINEERING GRADS

39% WOMEN
61% MEN

GENDER GAP 22%

2011
STEM WORK FORCE

76% MEN
24% WOMEN

GENDER GAP 52%

PERCENTAGE OF WOMEN IN STEM FROM 1970-2011

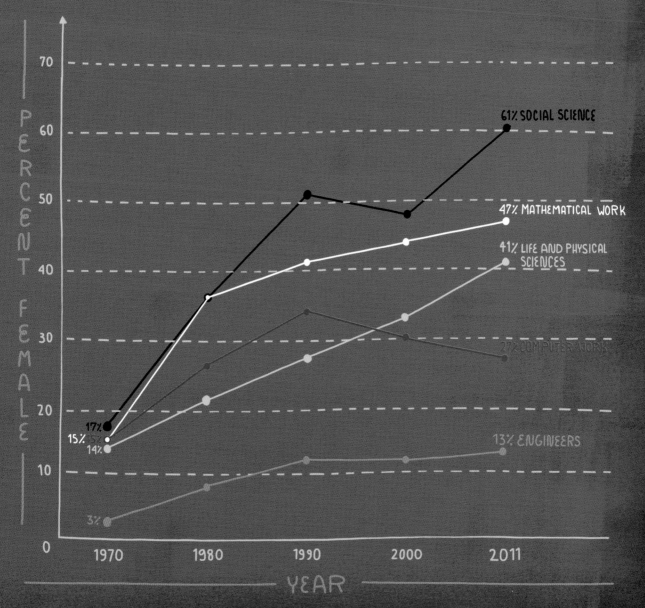

PERCENT FEMALE

70

60 — 61% SOCIAL SCIENCE

50

47% MATHEMATICAL WORK

41% LIFE AND PHYSICAL SCIENCES

40

30 — 27% COMPUTER WORK

20

17%
15% 15%
14%

13% ENGINEERS

10

3%

0

1970   1980   1990   2000   2011

YEAR

ELECTED TO THE NATIONAL ACADEMY OF SCIENCES.

WON THE NATIONAL MEDAL OF SCIENCE.

MADE BRAND NEW OBSERVATIONS ON HOW GALAXIES ROTATE.

DISCOVERED REAL PROOF THAT DARK MATTER EXISTS.

'STILL MORE MYSTERIES OF THE UNIVERSE REMAIN HIDDEN. THEIR DISCOVERY AWAITS THE ADVENTUROUS SCIENTISTS OF THE FUTURE. I LIKE IT THIS WAY.' —VERA RUBIN

VERA RUBIN

ASTRONOMER

Vera Rubin was born in 1928 in Philadelphia, and grew up in Washington, DC. She always had an interest in the night sky, looking up at the stars with her cardboard telescope.

Princeton University would not admit women to their graduate astronomy programme, so Vera went to Cornell instead. Aged 22 she made headlines with her theory that the universe is rotating. This is still under debate, but most evidence points to Vera being correct.

She later started work at the Carnegie Institution of Washington, where she met Kent Ford. He invented a new spectrometer that could be used to see light from distant stars. Vera used the spectrometer to start her work on spiral rotating galaxies. The theory was that galaxies spin the same way solar systems do. The farther away from a gravity point, the slower an object would move, just like the different speeds of planets circling the Sun.

Vera studied over 60 different spiral galaxies. In every one, she made the same observation: they rotated at the same speed! What was causing this? Vera connected her findings to Fritz Zwicky's theory about undetectable 'dark matter'. Dark matter was creating a gravitational pull that affected how objects moved in the universe. Although most astronomers didn't believe this invisible matter existed, Vera's findings could not be ignored. Her observations could be explained only by the presence of an undetectable mass. Dark matter makes up most of the universe, but it is still a mystery to scientists today.

Vera continues her research on the universe. She is always willing to mentor fellow female astronomers.

HER DAD HELPED HER BUILD HER FIRST TELESCOPE.

FIRST WOMAN TO USE THE PALOMAR OBSERVATORY WITHOUT SNEAKING IN.

HAD 4 KIDS — AND ALL OF THEM BECAME SCIENTISTS.

DISCOVERED A NEW GALAXY WITH TWO HALVES THAT ROTATE IN OPPOSITE DIRECTIONS.

WON THE JAMES CRAIG WATSON MEDAL FROM THE NATIONAL ACADEMY OF SCIENCES.

SO THAT'S WHAT WE LOOK LIKE!

WISHES SHE COULD VISIT ANDROMEDA AND LOOK BACK AT THE MILKY WAY.

DID IMPORTANT RESEARCH ON ALTERNATIVE ENERGY.

HELPED TO CREATE SOFTWARE FOR THE CENTAUR ROCKET.

CO-WROTE MANY PAPERS ABOUT NUCLEAR ROCKET ENGINES AND POWER PLANTS.

'NOTHING WAS GIVEN TO MINORITIES OR WOMEN. IT TOOK SOME FIGHTING TO GET THAT EQUAL OPPORTUNITY AND WE'RE STILL FIGHTING TODAY.' —ANNIE EASLEY

ANNIE EASLEY

COMPUTER PROGRAMMER, MATHEMATICIAN AND ROCKET SCIENTIST

Annie Easley was born in Alabama, USA in 1933. Living in the American south at that time meant being subjected to laws that tried to stop black people voting. Annie used her smarts to teach others how to pass a ridiculous voting test.

Annie always wanted to become a nurse, but when Cleveland State University's pharmacy programme shut down, she switched to maths – and became one of the first rocket scientists in America. She began by working as a human computer at NACA (soon to become NASA) in 1955. When NASA got mechanical computers, Annie used them as tools to start her work as a mathematician.

After the Russians launched Sputnik in 1957, NASA had all hands on deck working to get a rocket into space. In 1958, the Centaur project was developing a high-energy rocket launcher. Annie worked on one of the first computer programs to enable navigation in space. Since the 1960s, this upper stage of NASA rockets has been used in over 100 launches to get satellites and probes into space. The Centaur project is still considered some of NASA's most important research.

In the 1970s, NASA looked for new ways to create fuel, to solve the energy crisis. Annie researched power plants and electric batteries, creating a computer program that measured solar winds. Her work with electric batteries laid the foundation for today's hybrid cars.

Annie Easley understood that being flexible, believing in yourself and working hard can lead to amazing opportunities.

I BELIEVE IN YOU!

RAISED BY A SINGLE MUM WHO ALWAYS ENCOURAGED HER.

TRAVELLED TO CAPE CANAVERAL TO WATCH THE ROCKET LAUNCHES.

TUTORED UNDER-PRIVILEGED INNER-CITY KIDS IN HER FREE TIME.

WAS AN EQUAL OPPORTUNITY COUNSELLOR AND TAUGHT ABOUT WORKPLACE DISCRIMINATION.

PRESIDENT OF NASA'S SKIING CLUB.

ALSO WORKED IN THE LAUNCH VEHICLES DIVISION OF NASA.

EARNED A DEGREE IN MATHEMATICS FROM CLEVELAND STATE WHILE WORKING AT NASA.

UN MESSENGER OF PEACE.

THE WORLD'S FOREMOST EXPERT ON CHIMPANZEES.

DISCOVERED PRIMATE TOOL-MAKING.

ANIMAL RIGHTS AND WILDLIFE CONSERVATION ACTIVIST.

'ONLY WHEN OUR CLEVER BRAIN AND OUR HUMAN HEART WORK TOGETHER CAN WE REACH OUR FULL POTENTIAL.' —JANE GOODALL—

JANE GOODALL

PRIMATOLOGIST, ETHOLOGIST AND ANTHROPOLOGIST

THE BOOK TARZAN SPARKED HER DREAM TO GO TO AFRICA.

Jane Goodall was born in Britain in 1934. She longed to study wildlife in Africa, so she worked as a production assistant on documentaries and as a waitress, saving up for her dream. People said that travelling to Africa was too dangerous for a woman, but by pinching her pennies, Jane funded her way to Kenya. There she met Louis Leakey, a scientist studying prehistoric humans. He was impressed with Jane's knowledge of Africa and hired her. Louis wanted to study chimpanzees to see if they resembled primitive humans, and Jane's know-how made her the best person to go to Tanzania to live among the chimps.

The chimps did not trust Jane, but one she named David Greybeard overcame his fear and opened up to her. As the chimps grew used to her, she was able to document behaviours never seen before, such as using twigs as tools. Scientists used to think that only humans used tools; now we understand that chimps are more like us than we thought. After Jane's discovery, she was sponsored by the National Geographic Society to stay. Her research showed the world that chimps have complex social hierarchies, distinct personalities and capacity for both compassion and cruelty. They are socially and biologically very similar to humans.

Jane also knew that the chimps were in danger. Poverty had led local communities to eat chimps and destroy their habitats with bad farming practices. She started conservation organisations like the Jane Goodall Institute to help protect chimps and their habitat.

Jane continues to work today. She has changed the way we all understand animals – and ourselves.

NAMED ALL OF THE CHIMPS SHE STUDIED – THE MOST FAMOUS ARE DAVID GREYBEARD, GOLIATH & FLO.

NATIONAL GEOGRAPHIC TV SPECIALS ABOUT JANE MADE HER FAMOUS.

STILL HAS HER STUFFED MONKEY 'JUBILEE' FROM WHEN SHE WAS A CHILD.

THAT'S MY GIRL!

BROUGHT HER MUM ALONG ON HER FIRST STAY WITH THE CHIMPS.

SAW COMPASSION IN THE CHIMPS WHEN A MALE ADOPTED AN ORPHAN CHIMP AS HIS OWN.

FIGHTS TO CREATE A PROTECTED OCEAN TO STOP POLLUTION AND OVERFISHING.

IN THE JIM SUIT, SHE MADE THE DEEPEST DIVE IN 1979 & STILL HOLDS THE WOMEN'S DEPTH RECORD.

NATIONAL GEOGRAPHIC EXPLORER-IN-RESIDENCE.

HER RESEARCH, EXPLORATION & PHOTOGRAPHY HELP EDUCATE PEOPLE ABOUT THE WORLD'S OCEANS.

'NO WATER, NO LIFE. NO BLUE, NO GREEN.' — SYLVIA EARLE

SYLVIA EARLE

MARINE BIOLOGIST, EXPLORER AND AQUANAUT

Like an astronaut on the Moon, Sylvia Earle has set foot on a previously unexplored frontier: the ocean floor. She was born in 1935 in New Jersey, USA. In her quest to learn about the ocean, she became a marine biologist.

In 1966, Sylvia got a doctorate from Duke University, where much of her research focused on algae. She scuba-dived to collect over 20,000 algae samples to write her dissertation. She went on to be the first woman to dive out of the lockout chamber of a submerged submarine in 1968.

In 1969, a new underwater research lab called the Tektite Project was developed in which scientists could live for a few weeks – at a depth of 15 metres – in the Great Lameshur Bay in the Virgin Islands. This captured Sylvia's interest, but she could not join the all-male mission. She led the all-female Tektite II team the next year. She loved spending up to 10 hours diving among the coral reefs outside her Tektite home.

When Sylvia wasn't researching and writing books, she was exploring new depths (quite literally!). In 1979, she wore a person-sized submarine called the JIM suit and broke the depth record for an untethered dive. Deep in the Pacific Ocean, she observed luminescent animals. She went on to help develop the submarine *Deep Rover* and became a National Geographic explorer-in-residence.

Throughout her career, Sylvia has focused on the fight to save our oceans from overfishing and pollution. Through her lectures and underwater photography, she works to ensure a protected ocean.

NICKNAMED 'HER DEEPNESS' AND 'THE STURGEON GENERAL'.

TIME

NAMED TIME MAGAZINE'S FIRST 'HERO FOR THE PLANET' IN 1998.

MISSION BLUE

WITH 'MISSION BLUE' SHE IS CREATING PROTECTED PARTS OF THE OCEAN CALLED 'HOPE SPOTS'.

SHE WAS INSPIRED BY THE BOOK HALF MILE DOWN AND JACQUES COUSTEAU'S SCUBA FILMS.

HALF MILE DOWN

LED THE SUSTAINABLE SEAS EXPEDITIONS.

NOAA

WAS THE CHIEF SCIENTIST FOR NOAA BUT LEFT SO SHE COULD HAVE MORE FREEDOM TO SPEAK OUT ABOUT OVERFISHING.

FIRST WOMAN IN SPACE.

CONTINUES TO HELP TRAIN COSMONAUTS.

LOGGED MORE TIME IN SPACE THAN ANYONE ON PREVIOUS MISSIONS.

'ONCE YOU ARE AT THIS FARAWAY DISTANCE [IN SPACE], YOU REALISE THE SIGNIFICANCE OF WHAT IT IS THAT UNITES US. LET US WORK TOGETHER TO OVERCOME OUR DIFFERENCES.' —VALENTINA TERESHKOVA

VALENTINA TERESHKOVA

* ENGINEER AND COSMONAUT *

Valentina Tereshkova was born in 1937, in what is now Russia – at the time her country was the USSR. Her family was so poor that they couldn't afford bread. She worked in tyre and textile factories, but she dreamed of exploring the world.

When the space race between the United States and the USSR began, the USSR wanted to be first to send a woman into space. Valentina was in a parachute club, making her a perfect cosmonaut candidate. Valentina was selected to compete with four other women – she had to keep it a secret, even from her family. The training was intense, but Valentina was chosen to be the first woman in space.

Valentina flew solo into space on a shuttle called *Vostok VI* in 1963. She orbited the Earth 48 times, setting a new record. The photographs she took in space helped us gain a better understanding of the atmosphere.

She had a bumpy ride back to Earth when there were problems in the ship's programming. Nauseated and disoriented, Valentina manually corrected the error. She passed out, then woke up, bruised her nose and had to stand on her head to get out of her parachute when she landed.

Valentina showed the world that women are tough as nails. After her flight, she earned a doctorate in engineering and worked closely with the cosmonaut programme. Today she works for world peace.

AS A KID SHE WANTED TO TRAVEL THE USSR AS A TRAIN DRIVER.

HER OFFICIAL CALL SIGN WAS 'SEAGULL'.

PEOPLE BROUGHT HER MILK & POTATOES AT HER LANDING SITE.

HAS A LUNAR CRATER NAMED AFTER HER.

YELLED 'HELLO, SKY! TAKE OFF YOUR HAT, I AM ON MY WAY!' AS SHE FLEW UP INTO SPACE.

HER FIRST HUSBAND WAS COSMONAUT ANDRIYAN NIKOLAYEV, MAKING THEM THE FIRST COUPLE WHO HAVE BOTH BEEN IN SPACE.

HER NEW GOAL IS TO GO TO MARS.

PIONEERED VOLCANO NATURE PHOTOGRAPHY.

STARTED HER OWN FOUNDATION FOR VOLCANOLOGY WITH HUSBAND MAURICE KRAFFT.

USED OBSERVATIONS TO HELP GOVERNMENTS DEVELOP VOLCANO EVACUATION PROCEDURES.

'FOR ME THE DANGER IS NOT IMPORTANT ... ON VOLCANOES I FORGET EVERYTHING.' —KATIA KRAFFT

KATIA KRAFFT

GEOLOGIST AND VOLCANOLOGIST

Katia Krafft was born in 1942 in France. She fell in love with volcanoes when she saw pictures of them. She studied geology at the University of Strasbourg, where she met her husband and fellow volcano fanatic, Maurice.

Katia started her career by taking gas samples of volcanoes, and she and Maurice would observe erupting volcanoes in person. Volcanoes are dangerous, and many scientists were too afraid to do this, but not Maurice and Katia.

Their observations have led to a better understanding of volcanic eruptions. Together Maurice and Katia documented dangerous ash clouds, new volcanoes being formed and the effects of acid rain. They even went on a raft into a lake of acid to get proper readings. Their photography and videos allowed them to work with governments on safety procedures. One of their last videos was *Reducing Volcanic Risks*, but that didn't mean they stopped being daredevils. They continued to push the boundaries, going closer to the volcano and staying longer during an eruption. In 1991, their luck ran out, and Mount Unzen in Japan took their lives when the lava changed course.

Katia died doing what she loved with the person she loved. For years she studied volcanoes right at their edge. Her bravery and expertise have given us a greater understanding of volcanoes that will endure.

THE KRAFFT MEDAL IS NOW GIVEN OUT TO EXCEPTIONAL VOLCANOLOGISTS.

CLUNK

WORE A SPECIAL HELMET TO PROTECT HER SKULL FROM FALLING ROCKS.

PBS

MADE A DOCUMENTARY, THE VOLCANO WATCHERS, FOR THE PBS SHOW NATURE.

KATIA AND MAURICE STARTED THEIR OWN VOLCANO CENTRE IN 1968.

TOGETHER THE KRAFFTS WROTE MANY BOOKS THAT FUNDED THEIR TRIPS ALL OVER THE WORLD.

WAS KILLED BY A PYROCLASTIC FLOW THAT CHANGED DIRECTION.

USED MUTATED FRUIT FLIES TO UNDERSTAND HOW GENES INSTRUCT STEM CELLS TO GROW.

CONTRIBUTED TO THE UNDERSTANDING OF EVOLUTION AND HOW HUMAN FOETUSES DEVELOP.

WON A NOBEL PRIZE IN PHYSIOLOGY OR MEDICINE FOR HER WORK IN GENETICS.

'I IMMEDIATELY LOVED WORKING WITH FLIES. THEY FASCINATED ME, AND FOLLOWED ME AROUND IN MY DREAMS.' —CHRISTIANE NÜSSLEIN-VOLHARD

CHRISTIANE NÜSSLEIN-VOLHARD

BIOLOGIST

DEVELOPED A BLOCK SYSTEM FOR COLLECTING FLY EMBRYOS.

HAS AROUND 500,000 ZEBRA FISH FOR HER GENETIC RESEARCH.

STUDIED A MUTANT FLY WITH NO HEAD AND TWO TAILS.

Christiane Nüsslein-Volhard was born in Germany in 1942. She knew she wanted to be a biologist from the age of 12 and became intensely focused on pursuing her goal.

At the time, men greatly outnumbered women at universities in Germany, and women were expected to stay at home. It was a very competitive environment, but Christiane prevailed. After completing her PhD in molecular biology, she decided to focus on genetics.

Christiane worked with *Drosophila*, also known as fruit flies. She was mesmerised by their development: how does a fertilised cell become a complicated animal? How do genes instruct our cells to grow? She began harvesting fly embryos and exposing them to mutagens. She would then see which part of the fly was affected by the mutation. Christiane and her team found success: they were able to see which genes were involved in the embryo's pattern formation and which genes determined the fly's body plan and segmentation. She won the 1995 Nobel Prize in physiology or medicine.

This research led directly to us understanding how human embryos develop, and to learning more about the evolution of species. Her work paved the way for doctors to be able to screen for birth defects and understand what can cause miscarriages.

She now uses zebra fish to research mutated genes. She is happy to share her mutant fish with other researchers upon request.

LOVED GARDENING AND COLLECTED SNAILS AND BUGS AS A KID.

LADY OF THE FLIES

NEWSPAPERS CALLED HER 'LADY OF THE FLIES' AND 'DAME DROSOPHILA'.

HAD DREAMS ABOUT FRUIT FLIES.

THE CHRISTIANE NÜSSLEIN-VOLHARD FOUNDATION HELPS WOMEN SCIENTISTS PAY FOR DAYCARE.

INVENTOR OF THE LASERPHACO PROBE USED TO TREAT CATARACTS.

PIONEERED VOLUNTEER-BASED OUTREACH TO BRING EYE CARE TO IMPOVERISHED PEOPLE.

CO-FOUNDER OF THE AMERICAN INSTITUTE FOR THE PREVENTION OF BLINDNESS.

'BELIEVE IN THE POWER OF TRUTH ... DO NOT ALLOW YOUR MIND TO BE IMPRISONED BY MAJORITY THINKING.' – PATRICIA BATH

PATRICIA BATH

OPHTHALMOLOGIST AND INVENTOR

Patricia Bath was born in 1942 in New York City. She finished high school in under three years and helped with cancer research when she was only 16. She was bound to change the world.

Patricia was no stranger to racism or sexism. She didn't know any female doctors, and many of the medical schools were for whites only. Despite this, Patricia knew she wanted to be a doctor. After earning her degree at Howard University, she became a fellow at Columbia University.

Her research showed that African-Americans were more prone to certain vision problems, such as glaucoma. People living in poor communities could not afford regular eye care, so relatively minor eye problems could lead to blindness. Patricia couldn't just stand by and watch this injustice, so she started the first community outreach eye-care programme – convincing a fellow surgeon to operate on patients for free. She went on to co-found the American Institute for the Prevention of Blindness (AiPB).

Patricia became a professor at UCLA. She was the first female faculty member at the ophthalmology school and often did not get the respect she deserved from her peers. After becoming the chair of the training programme, she travelled to Europe to do research.

In 1986, she finished inventing the Laserphaco Probe, which removes cataracts. It was a major breakthrough that helped restore the sight of many people. Patricia continues to work with the AiPB, taking preventative eye care and sight-restoring surgery around the globe.

PATRICIA'S MUM BOUGHT HER FIRST CHEMISTRY SET.

ORGANISED THE FIRST MAJOR EYE SURGERY FOR HARLEM HOSPITAL IN 1970.

VACCINATED CHILDREN IN DEVELOPING COUNTRIES AGAINST THE MEASLES.

WAS INSPIRED TO BECOME A DOCTOR BY DR ALBERT SCHWEITZER'S WORK WITH LEPROSY.

VITAMIN EYE DROPS FOR BABIES

FIRST AFRICAN-AMERICAN TO COMPLETE A RESIDENCY IN OPHTHALMOLOGY.

FIRST AFRICAN-AMERICAN WOMAN TO GET A MEDICAL PATENT IN 1998.

CO-FOUNDED THE AMERICAN INSTITUTE FOR THE PREVENTION OF BLINDNESS.

I CAN SEE!

SHE RESTORED SIGHT IN PEOPLE WHO HAD BEEN BLIND FOR DECADES.

DISCOVERED A NEW TYPE OF STAR: A PULSAR.

CONTINUES TO STUDY STARS AND BLACK HOLES.

HER RESEARCH GAVE US A FURTHER UNDERSTANDING OF THE LIFE CYCLE OF STARS AND PLANETS.

'IF WE ASSUME WE'VE ARRIVED [AT ABSOLUTE TRUTH], WE STOP SEARCHING. WE STOP DEVELOPING.' —JOCELYN BELL BURNELL

JOCELYN BELL BURNELL

ASTROPHYSICIST

Jocelyn Bell Burnell was born in 1943 in Ireland. When her school wouldn't let girls into the science lab, her parents protested until she was allowed in the class. Jocelyn got the best grades.

She was one of very few women in the physics department at Glasgow University. Every time she entered a science lecture, her male classmates would catcall her and make comments about her appearance. She held her head up high and graduated in 1965 with honours. She was accepted to the University of Cambridge's graduate programme and finished her doctorate there in 1969.

At Cambridge she helped build a large radio telescope. She was also in charge of interpreting printouts of radio transmissions coming from space. One night, she noticed radio waves pulsing from deep space on the readouts. Her advisers thought it could be a signal from alien life, but Jocelyn saw radio waves in different places in the sky, proving that it was a natural occurrence. The waves came from a small and dense star called a pulsar, which throws out beams of radiation like a lighthouse. Jocelyn's work helped her adviser, Antony Hewish, win a Nobel Prize.

Jocelyn still researches stars and black holes. She wants everyone to know that all elements come from exploding stars, so we 'are made of star stuff'.

DISCOVERED PULSARS AT THE AGE OF 24.

THE PULSAR SIGNAL WAS NICKNAMED 'LGM' OR LITTLE GREEN MEN.

HAD A CHILDHOOD CAT NAMED 'VOSTOK', AFTER THE FIRST SATELLITES.

SHE WAS THE PRESIDENT OF THE ROYAL ASTRONOMICAL SOCIETY 2002-2004.

nature

HER DISCOVERY WAS PUBLISHED IN THE SCIENCE JOURNAL NATURE.

SHE ADVOCATES FOR MORE WOMEN IN SCIENCE.

SAU LAN WU

PARTICLE PHYSICIST

Sau Lan Wu was born in the early 1940s, during the Japanese occupation of Hong Kong. Against her father's wishes, she applied to 50 universities in America. She attended Vassar College with a full scholarship and was accepted into Harvard's masters programme in physics – the only woman admitted that year.

VASSAR COLLEGE

After earning a PhD from Harvard, Sau Lan Wu started researching particle physics – the study of matter and how it works. Atoms are made of protons and neutrons, which are made of quarks. Sau Lan Wu was fascinated by these particles and dedicated her life to discovering their secrets.

With a research team led by Samuel Ting, Sau Lan Wu helped to discover the charm quark, a type of elementary particle, in 1974. She then became the lead on a research team that discovered the gluon, a particle that holds quarks together.

One unanswered question in physics was how the tiny particles that make up an atom have any mass. In 1964, a theory that mass depended on a subatomic particle called the Higgs boson was created. To prove this theory, researchers had to find a Higgs boson. Sau Lan Wu said, 'It is like looking for a needle in a haystack – the size of a football stadium.' With a particle accelerator, Wu led one of the teams finding proof of these teeny particles. In 2012, her team was instrumental in observing the Higgs boson.

Sau Lan Wu is one of the most important particle physicists in her field. She continues to discover what all the stuff in the universe is made of.

THE LARGE HADRON COLLIDER PARTICLE ACCELERATOR IS 27 KM LONG.

EPS

WON THE EUROPEAN PHYSICAL SOCIETY PRIZE FOR HIGH-ENERGY PHYSICS IN 1995.

FELLOW OF THE AMERICAN ACADEMY OF ARTS AND SCIENCES.

SHE HAS MET HER OWN PERSONAL GOAL TO MAKE AT LEAST THREE MAJOR DISCOVERIES.

THE HIGGS BOSON IS CALLED THE 'GOD PARTICLE'.

SUMMER SCHOOL AT THE BROOKHAVEN NATIONAL LABORATORY INTRODUCED HER TO PARTICLE PHYSICS.

HER HERO IS HER MOTHER.

A BIOGRAPHY OF MARIE CURIE INSPIRED HER TO BECOME A SCIENTIST.

ELIZABETH BLACKBURN

MOLECULAR BIOLOGIST

Elizabeth Blackburn was born in 1948 in Australia. A childhood love of animals led to her passion for biology.

After Elizabeth completed her master's degree, she left home to earn a PhD in the UK. At the University of Cambridge, she studied DNA sequences of bacteriophages. She was thrilled to be working with DNA, the key to understanding how all life works. She went to America to continue pursuing research in her new favourite subject.

In the 1970s, no one really knew what the ends of chromosomes were like. Chromosomes are tightly wound DNA material that tell our body's cells what to do. Elizabeth wanted to understand how they worked.

She noticed that there were special kinds of DNA called telomeres on each end of the chromosomes that worked as protective caps. She discovered that telomeres are made of nonessential segments of DNA that break off every time a cell divides, protecting the important information. When we get older, this protective cap wears out and our chromosomes get damaged. This loss of DNA causes our cells to work incorrectly or die, leading to diseases like cancer and Alzheimer's.

Elizabeth wanted to understand what keeps our telomeres healthy. In 1984, with the help of her student Carol Greider, she co-discovered telomerase, an enzyme that rebuilds telomeres to a healthy length. In 2009, she was awarded the Nobel Prize in physiology or medicine.

Elizabeth's research shows that a healthy telomere length is needed for living a long, healthy life. She studies the science behind longevity to this day.

EXERCISE, SLEEP, LOW STRESS LEVELS AND HEALTHY DIET ARE PROVEN TO HELP KEEP TELOMERES HEALTHY.

WORKED AT YALE, UC SAN FRANCISCO AND UC BERKELEY.

I'M POND SCUM!

WORKED WITH A PROTOZOAN CALLED TETRAHYMENA TO STUDY TELOMERES.

WAS THE PRESIDENT OF THE AMERICAN SOCIETY FOR CELL BIOLOGY IN 1998.

TIME
100

WAS IN THE 2007 PUBLICATION OF 'THE TIME 100 — THE PEOPLE WHO SHAPED OUR WORLD' IN TIME MAGAZINE.

ELIZABETH MET BARBARA MCCLINTOCK, WHO TOLD HER TO TRUST HER OWN INTUITION!

PRINCIPAL OF THE 100 YEAR STARSHIP PROJECT.

FIRST AFRICAN-AMERICAN WOMAN IN SPACE.

FOUNDER OF JEMISON GROUP INC. AND BIOSENTIENT CORPORATION.

'THE FIRST THING ABOUT EMPOWERMENT IS TO UNDERSTAND THAT YOU HAVE THE RIGHT TO BE INVOLVED. THE SECOND ONE IS THAT YOU HAVE SOMETHING IMPORTANT TO CONTRIBUTE. AND THE THIRD PIECE IS THAT YOU HAVE TO TAKE THE RISK TO CONTRIBUTE IT.' – MAE JEMISON

MAE JEMISON

ASTRONAUT, EDUCATOR, AND DOCTOR

Mae Jemison always knew she would go into space. She was born in 1956 in the USA. She was obsessed with the Apollo missions but noticed that there was no one who looked like her going into space. However, the fictional TV show *Star Trek* featured people of different genders and races working together. Lieutenant Uhura became her role model.

FOUND OUT SHE WAS GOING TO BE AN ASTRONAUT IN BETWEEN GIVING MEDICAL EXAMINATIONS.

HER DAD TAUGHT HER HOW TO COUNT CARDS AS A KID.

WENT ON AN EIGHT-DAY MISSION IN SPACE.

THE FIRST LANDMARK SHE IDENTIFIED FROM SPACE WAS CHICAGO, HER HOMETOWN.

DID EXPERIMENTS WITH BONE CELLS WHILE IN SPACE.

WON A SCHOLARSHIP TO STANFORD WHEN SHE WAS 16.

WAS FEATURED ON AN EPISODE OF STAR TREK: THE NEXT GENERATION.

FOUNDED 'THE EARTH WE SHARE' SCIENCE CAMP FOR KIDS.

SHE IS A DANCER.

Mae did her undergraduate degree at Stanford University in chemical engineering and African-American studies. She went on to Cornell and became a doctor, working in the Peace Corps in Africa for several years. When it was time to chase her space dream, Mae applied to NASA and became an astronaut.

In 1992, Mae Jemison became the first African-American woman in space. On the shuttle *Endeavour*, she took objects from African and African-American culture so black people would be represented in space.

The following year, she left NASA and started numerous companies, including a technology consulting firm, the Jemison Group Inc., and the BioSentient Corporation, which creates devices to allow doctors to monitor patients' day-to-day nervous system functions.

Mae is also principal of the 100 Year Starship project, which aims for human travel to the next solar system within 100 years. This project will also inspire new types of materials, recycling, energy and fuel. Mae still has her eyes on the stars while helping solve problems on Earth.

STAR TREK

A K A

CO-FOUNDER OF KAVLI INSTITUTE

DISCOVERED GRID CELLS AND HOW MAPS ARE MADE IN THE HUMAN MIND.

WON A NOBEL PRIZE IN PHYSIOLOGY OR MEDICINE WITH HER HUSBAND EDVARD.

'A GOOD DESIGNER HAS A LOT IN COMMON WITH A GOOD RESEARCHER. BOTH HUNT FOR EXCELLENCE AND PERFECTION. AND YOU HAVE TO REALLY FOCUS ON THE DETAILS, AND YOU DON'T REALLY KNOW WHAT THE FINAL RESULT WILL BE BEFORE YOU HAVE IT.' —MAY-BRITT MOSER

MAY-BRITT MOSER

PSYCHOLOGIST AND NEUROSCIENTIST

May-Britt Moser was born in 1963 in Norway. She went to the University of Oslo and studied psychology. There, she became good friends with Edvard Moser, a boy she knew from high school. They fell in love, got married and went on to become research partners. The couple graduated with PhDs in neurophysiology in 1995.

The workings of the human brain are still a bit of a mystery. Simple tasks, such as remembering where we are and the route to get home, pose complicated questions about how memory forms and where information is stored in the brain. May-Britt and Edvard wanted to answer these questions and understand how humans navigate. Their experiments focused on rats going through mazes while their brain activity was monitored.

In 2005, Edvard and May-Britt discovered a new type of nerve cell called grid cells. As a rat moved through a maze, a 'co-ordinate' map was being created in its brain out of these grid cells. That is how the rat could orient itself.

Every time we go somewhere new, we use these grid cells to create a map like a GPS system. When our grid cells are damaged, we become very forgetful. Grid cells are crucial to our memory, and understanding them can help us treat memory-related illnesses such as Alzheimer's.

May-Britt and Edvard have opened a new door to understanding the ways our brains process information. Together, in 2014 they won a Nobel Prize in physiology or medicine. May-Britt continues to study the human brain and unlock its secrets.

GRID CELLS IN OUR BRAIN ARE ALL EVENLY ARRANGED IN TRIANGLES AND HEXAGONS.

WOW! SMELLS JUST LIKE GRANDMA!

SHE PUBLISHED A PAPER ON HOW SMELLS ACTIVATE MEMORIES.

HER MUM READ HER FAIRY TALES IN WHICH HEROES USED THEIR BRAINS.

SHE STUDIES HOW STRESS CAUSES MEMORY LOSS.

MAY-BRITT AND EDVARD HAVE TWO DAUGHTERS.

WORE A DRESS WITH EMBROIDERED GRID CELLS TO RECEIVE HER NOBEL PRIZE.

HAS DONE IMPORTANT WORK IN HYPERBOLIC GEOMETRY

FIRST WOMAN TO WIN THE FIELDS MEDAL.

HAS GIVEN US NEW INSIGHT INTO THE DYNAMICS OF ABSTRACT SURFACES.

'YOU HAVE TO SPEND SOME ENERGY AND EFFORT TO SEE THE BEAUTY OF MATH.' — MARYAM MIRZAKHANI

MARYAM MIRZAKHANI

MATHEMATICIAN

Maryam Mirzakhani, born in 1977 in Iran, grew up reading every book she could find. In high school, she got her hands on the entrance questionnaire for a maths competition. Maryam spent days on a worksheet that should have only taken her hours. She demanded that her all-girl school provide a maths course equal to the boys' schools'.

Maryam came to America for graduate school at Harvard. She became interested in understanding the surface of a shape and what happens when it is distorted. She enjoyed finding the beauty in mathematics and focused on hyperbolic surfaces. Hyperbolic doughnuts are abstract shapes; to understand them, you need to find straight lines inside them. This is incredibly difficult. Maryam created an equation that showed the relationship between the number of straight lines and the length of the side of a hyperbolic structure. Her work is essential to understanding curved shapes and surfaces.

There was another unsolved problem in mathematics: if a billiard ball is bouncing around, hitting the sides of a table in a frictionless environment, will the ball always end up where it started? What about the infinite possible shapes of the billiard table? This problem was so complicated, computers couldn't even simulate it! Maryam solved it. Instead of moving the ball around the table, she mirrored the table around the ball, which helped her figure out that the ball will always close its loop. This has given us a better understanding of geometry and physics.

In 2014, Maryam won the Fields Medal for her work, the first woman so honoured. She continues to push boundaries in mathematics.

THE FIELDS MEDAL IS CONSIDERED THE NOBEL PRIZE IN MATHS.

HAS DONE IMPORTANT WORK ON TEICHMÜLLER DYNAMICS AND MODULI SPACE.

MARYAM AND HER FRIEND BECAME THE FIRST GIRLS ON IRAN'S INTERNATIONAL MATHEMATICAL OLYMPIAD TEAM AND SHE WON A GOLD MEDAL.

$$\frac{N(N+1)}{2}$$

AS A CHILD SHE WAS INSPIRED WHEN HER OLDER BROTHER TOLD HER ABOUT THE MATHS PROBLEM OF ADDING ALL THE NUMBERS BETWEEN 1 AND 100.

CREATED A NEW PROOF OF EDWARD WITTEN'S THEORY ABOUT TOPOLOGICAL MEASUREMENTS OF MODULI SPACES.

SHE DRAWS HYPERBOLIC SHAPES ON HUGE PIECES OF PAPER TO BETTER UNDERSTAND THEM.

MORE WOMEN IN SCIENCE

IRÈNE JOLIOT-CURIE
1897-1956

Marie Curie's daughter and Nobel Prize winner. Chemist who created synthetic radioactive elements.

JANAKI AMMAL
1897-1984

Worked at the Botanical Survey of India and did important work on crossbreeding sugar cane.

ANNA JANE HARRISON
1912-1998

Studied how atoms become molecules. American Chemical Society's first woman president.

SHIRLEY ANN JACKSON
1946-

President of Rensselaer Polytechnic Institute. First black person to earn a PhD from MIT.

LINDA BUCK
1947-

Won Nobel Prize in physiology or medicine for work on how we use our olfactory nerves.

FRANÇOISE BARRE-SINOUSSI
1947-

Virologist who won Nobel Prize in physiology or medicine for her discovery of HIV.

MARIA MITCHELL
1818-1889

First American woman to work as an astronomer. Discovered 'Miss Mitchell's Comet'.

EMILY ROEBLING
1843-1903

American field engineer responsible for building the Brooklyn Bridge.

SOFIA KOVALEVSKAYA
1850-1891

Worked on partial differential maths equations. Created Cauchy-Kovalevskaya theorem.

MARY LEAKEY
1913-1996

Her fossil discoveries of our ancient ancestors changed our understanding of man's evolution.

EDITH FLANIGEN
1929-

Chemist who invented a synthetic emerald, and molecular sieves to process crude oil and purify water.

ADA YONATH
1939-

Israeli crystallographer who discovered ribosome structure. Won Nobel Prize in chemistry.

SALLY RIDE
1951-2012

First American woman in space and director of the California Space Institute.

TESSY THOMAS
1963 -

Indian engineer instrumental in creating the most powerful long-range nuclear missile.

THE NEXT GREAT SCIENTIST COULD BE YOU!

Women everywhere are working hard, learning and researching to make the next big breakthrough.

CONCLUSION

Women make up half of our population, and we simply cannot afford to ignore that brain power – the progress of humankind depends on our continual search for knowledge. The women in this book prove to the world that no matter your gender, your race or your background, anyone can achieve great things. Their legacy lives on. Women all over the world are still risking everything to discover and explore.

Let us celebrate these trailblazers so we can inspire the next generation. Together, we can pick up where they left off and continue the search for knowledge.

So go out and tackle new problems, find your answers and learn everything you can to make your own discoveries!

GLOSSARY

ABOLITIONIST

An activist working to end slavery and the slave trade.

ANTIVIRALS

Drugs to specifically fight viral infections.

ATOM

The smallest unit of matter. The centre, or nucleus, is made out of positive protons and neutral neutrons. The nucleus is surrounded by negatively charged electrons flying around. When different kinds of atoms combine, they make molecules.

BACTERIA

A type of single-celled organism found everywhere. There are many different kinds and they can be useful, harmful or helpful to plants and animals. For example, some make us sick, some help us digest our food and some help turn milk into cheese.

BACTERIOPHAGE

A virus that attacks and infects bacteria and then reproduces inside of it.

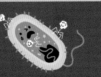

BETA DECAY

A type of radioactive decay of an atom in which a proton changes into a neutron (or vice versa) and a beta particle is emitted.

BOTANY

The study of plants.

CELL

The smallest unit of life. It can live on its own or be a building block for tissues to create organs in plants and animals.

CHROMOSOME

Tightly wound strands of DNA bundled together. They tell cells how to work.

COMPILER

A computer program that translates a computer language, such as COBOL, into something machines can understand.

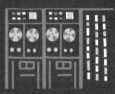

DNA

This molecular strand is our genetic instructions. It is inherited from our parents and tells our cells and bodies how to grow, reproduce and function. All organisms have DNA, and the strands are found in the nucleus of each cell.

ECLIPSE

A phenomenon that happens when three objects in space line up and the one in the middle blocks the view or light of one outer object from reaching the other.

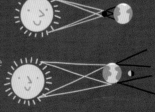

For example, in a lunar eclipse, the Earth aligns between Moon and Sun, casting its shadow on to the Moon and blocking the Sun's light; in a solar eclipse, the Moon aligns between Earth and Sun, casting its shadow on to the Earth and blocking the view of the Sun and its light from the Earth.

ECOSYSTEM

A group of organisms living together and their interaction with each other and the air, water and soil around them.

ELECTRIC ARCS

When two electrical currents ionise the gas or air around or between them, it creates a plasma discharge. They can now move through the air, which normally does not conduct electricity. Lightning is an example of a naturally occurring electric arc.

ELEMENT

In chemistry, a substance made up of only one kind of atom – such as gold or helium.

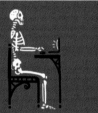

ERGONOMICS

The study of how people interact with tools and their environment. Ergonomics helps in the design of tools that work comfortably with how our bodies move.

FOSSIL

The remains of ancient animals and plants that have been preserved or even petrified over time. Sometimes the fossil, such as an old dinosaur bone, is stuck in a rock. Sometimes it is an imprint in the rock, like a footprint.

FREUDIAN THEORY

Part of a branch of social science called psychiatry. Named after the father of modern psychoanalysis, Sigmund Freud. It is a theory of how our unconscious desires interact with our consciously chosen actions.

TELL ME ABOUT YOUR DREAM

GENETICS

The study of how our DNA, chromosomes and genes work, how the genes that are passed down from our ancestors and parents change over time, and how they affect organisms.

GEOMORPHOLOGY

The study of how the surface of the Earth has changed over the span of its existence: for example, how mountains and continents form.

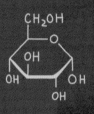

GLUCOSE

A sugar molecule that is an important source of energy for people. For example, when you eat a doughnut, all the sugars and carbohydrates are digested and broken down into glucose.

CH_2OH

OH

OH OH

OH

HERPETOLOGY

The study of reptiles and amphibians.

HUMAN COMPUTER

Before we had mechanical computers, complicated maths equations were done by a large group of people. Each person got a small part of the equation, and together they could solve the problem.

ISOTOPES

Created when the amount of neutrons in an atomic nucleus changes. There can be many different isotopes of the same atom, all with a different atomic mass but with the same number of protons.

INSULIN

The hormone that lets our body process sugar, or glucose, for energy and storage.

KOMODO DRAGON

The largest species of lizard, which can be very dangerous and venomous. It is native to Indonesia.

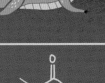

LACTIC ACID

A molecule created in our muscles when we exercise. It is created during the Cori cycle, described by Gerty and Carl Cori.

THE MANHATTAN PROJECT

A top-secret project created by the USA during the Second World War to develop the atomic bomb.

METAMORPHOSIS

Process in which an animal changes dramatically from one life stage to another – for example, a caterpillar using a cocoon to become a butterfly.

MODULI SPACE

Some maths problems have more than one answer. The set of all the possible answers to a geometry problem is called the moduli space.

MUTATIONS

A permanent change in the sequence of genes in an organism. It can happen while a cell is dividing its DNA during reproduction, when parts can be deleted or added to the code.

NASA

The US National Aeronautics and Space Administration.

NERVE CELLS

Also known as neurons, these are the cells that send information to our brain through chemical and electrical signals. They allow us to feel sensations, have thoughts, and they tell our bodies to move.

NERVE GROWTH FACTOR

A protein important for growing new cells and repairing and maintaining our nerve cells. It circulates throughout our entire body and is important for our survival.

NOBEL PRIZE

An annual prize in the subjects of physics, chemistry, physiology or medicine, literature, economics and peace. It is seen globally as one of the most prestigious prizes.

NOETHER THEORY

Proved that whenever there is a physical action that involves a predictable symmetry, it is because there is a law of conservation (for example, of mass, energy, momentum etc.).

PARTICLE ACCELERATOR

Uses an electromagnetic field to make particles move at super-fast speeds and smash apart when they collide with each other.

PULSARS

A neutron star that emits a beam of electromagnetic radiation. The beams come out of the magnetic poles of the star, and, as the star rotates, the beam pulses like a lighthouse.

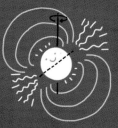

PUNCH CARDS

Literally a piece of stiff paper with holes punched into it in different places, creating code. It was one of the first methods of talking to a machine or a computer.

QUARKS

A type of subatomic particle that makes composite particles. In fact, they create neutrons and protons. Today we know six kinds of quarks, called flavours: up, down, strange, charm, bottom and top. There is still a lot to be discovered about quarks.

RADIOACTIVITY

The energy released when the atomic nucleus changes or becomes unstable. This release can include alpha particles, beta particles, gamma rays and electromagnetic waves.

RADIATION TECHNOLOGY

Radiation technology is used to see broken bones and in cancer treatment, but too much radiation exposure can cause cancer or radiation poisoning.

RING THEORY

The study of 'rings'. In maths, rings are sets of numbers where addition and multiplication are defined.

SOCIAL HIERARCHY

How animals or humans organise themselves to establish dominance and access to food and resources.

SPECTROSCOPE

An instrument that uses a prism to break light into the rainbow of colours across the electromagnetic spectrum.
It is used in astronomy and chemistry because atoms absorb light at different frequencies. By breaking up the light, measuring the different intensity and wavelengths, and looking for black line breaks, a scientist can pick out different atoms.

STELLAR SPECTRA

The rainbow of light and dark breaks seen from a star when looking through a spectroscope.

SUFFRAGIST

An activist who fought for voting rights for women.

VIRUS

Infectious agent, smaller than a cell. It can reproduce only by infecting other cells, in doing so causing diseases.

X-RAY CRYSTALLOGRAPHY

A tool that uses an X-ray beam on a crystal version of a substance. The beam goes in many different directions. By measuring the angles of the beams, scientists can understand the three-dimensional structures of different molecules and atoms.

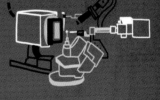

121

SOURCES

Researching this book was so much fun. I used all sorts of sources: newspapers, interviews, lectures, books, films and the internet! If you are interested in learning more about these women (and you should!), here are some of the sources I consulted. For more resources on the specific women featured in this book, go to www.rachelignotofskydesign.com/women-in-science/resources.

FILMS

Beautiful Minds: Jocelyn Bell Burnell. Directed by Jacqui Farnham. BBC Four, 2010. Series 1, episode 1 of 3.

Commencement Address: From Vassar to the Discovery of the Higgs Particle. Performed by Sau Lan Wu. Vassar College, 2014. commencement.vassar.edu/ceremony/2014/address/.

The Genius of Marie Curie. Directed by Gideon Bradshaw. BBC, 2013.

Great Floridians Film Series–Marjory Stoneman Douglas. By Marilyn Russell. Florida Department of State, 1987.

Jane Goodall at Concordia: Sowing the Seeds of Hope. Concordia University, 2014. www.youtube.com/watch?v=vibssrQKm60.

May-Britt and Edvard Moser – Winner of the Körber European Science Prize 2014. Directed by Axel Wagner. Koerber-Stiftung, 2014. www.youtube.com/watch?v=592ebE5U7c8.

Mission Blue. Directed by Robert Nixon and Fisher Stevens. Insurgent Media, 2014.

Signals: The Queen of Code. Directed by Gillian Jacobs. FiveThirtyEight, 2015. fivethirtyeight.com/features/the-queen-of-code/.

Valentina Tereshkova: Seagull in Space. Russia Today, 2013. www.youtube.com/watch?v=Y2k9s-NbNaA.

The Volcano Watchers. Directed by David Heeley. PBS, 1987.

WEBSITES

American Museum of Natural History: www.amnh.org
Encyclopedia Britannica: www.britannica.com
Jewish Women's Archive: www.jwa.org/encyclopedia
MAKERS, The largest video collection of women's stories: www.makers.com
NASA: www.nasa.gov
National Inventors Hall of Fame: www.invent.org
National Women's History Museum : www.nwhm.org
The Official Website of the Nobel Prize: www.nobelprize.org
Psychology's Feminist Voices: www.feministvoices.com
US National Library of Medicine: www.nlm.nih.gov/changingthefaceofmedicine

BOOKS

Adams, Katherine H. and Michael L. Keene. 2010. *After the Vote Was Won: The Later Achievements of Fifteen Suffragists*. Jefferson, NC: McFarland.

Layne, Margaret. 2009. *Women in Engineering*. Reston, VA: ASCE Press.

Dzielska, Maria. 1995. *Hypatia of Alexandria*. Cambridge, MA: Harvard University Press.

McGrayne, Sharon Bertsch. 1993. *Nobel Prize Women in Science: Their Lives, Struggles, and Momentous Disc*overies. Secaucus, NJ: Carol Publishing Group.

Peterson, Barbara Bennett. 2015. *Notable Women of China: Shang Dynasty to the Early Twentieth Century*. Oxford, UK: Routledge.

Swaby, Rachel. 2015. *Headstrong: 52 Women Who Changed Science—And the World*. New York: Broadway Books.

ACKNOWLEDGEMENTS

I first want to thank all of the women who are working in science now. Through their passion and hard work they are creating a better future. And, of course, thank you to the women who are staying up way too late studying and researching to become the best doctors, scientists and engineers they can be. I also want to thank all the young girls who are playing with bugs, looking at the stars and driving their parents nuts by taking apart old machines.

Special thanks to Thomas Mason IV for all of his love, support, amazing suggestions and bagels while I was creating this book. Thanks to Mia Mercado for all her grammar know-how. Another very special thank you for Aditya Voleti for helping me understand all of the maths in this book, and for his great suggestions, expert grammar skills, help with fact checking, and of course his very delicious biryani.

A special thank you to my editor, Kaitlin Ketchum, book designers Angelina Cheney and Tatiana Pavlova and the rest of the talented publishing team at Ten Speed Press for all of their hard work and expertise! And lastly, a big thank you to my literary agent Monica Odom for finding my work and believing in me.

ABOUT THE AUTHOR

Rachel Ignotofsky grew up in New Jersey, USA on a healthy diet of cartoons and pudding. She graduated with honours from Tyler School of Art's graphic design programme in 2011. Now she lives in beautiful Kansas City, Missouri, where she spends all day drawing and learning as much as she can. She has a passion for taking dense information and making it fun and accessible and is dedicated to creating educational works of art.

Rachel is inspired by history and science and believes that illustration is a powerful tool that can make learning exciting. She uses her work to spread her message about education, scientific literacy and powerful women. She hopes this book inspires girls and women to follow their passions and dreams.

This is Rachel's first book and she plans on writing many more in the future. To see more of Rachel's educational art and learn more about her, please visit www.rachelignotofskydesign.com.

INDEX

DEDICATED TO MY MOM AND DAD.

PUBLISHED IN GREAT BRITAIN IN 2017 BY WREN & ROOK
FIRST PUBLISHED IN THE UNITED STATES IN 2016 BY TEN SPEED PRESS

COPYRIGHT © 2016 RACHEL IGNOTOFSKY
PUBLISHED BY ARRANGEMENT WITH TEN SPEED PRESS, A DIVISION OF CROWN PUBLISHING

ISBN: 978 1 5263 6051 9
EBOOK ISBN: 978 1 5263 6063 2
10 9 8 7 6 5 4 3

MIX
Paper from
responsible sources
FSC® C104740

WREN & ROOK
AN IMPRINT OF
HACHETTE CHILDREN'S GROUP
PART OF HODDER & STOUGHTON
CARMELITE HOUSE
50 VICTORIA EMBANKMENT
LONDON EC4Y 0DZ

AN HACHETTE UK COMPANY
WWW.HACHETTE.CO.UK
WWW.HACHETTECHILDRENS.CO.UK

PRINTED IN ITALY

THE WEBSITE ADDRESSES (URLS) INCLUDED IN THIS
BOOK WERE VALID AT THE TIME OF GOING TO PRESS.
HOWEVER, IT IS POSSIBLE THAT CONTENTS OR ADDRESSES
MAY HAVE CHANGED SINCE THE PUBLICATION OF THIS
BOOK. NO RESPONSIBILITY FOR ANY SUCH CHANGES CAN
BE ACCEPTED BY EITHER THE AUTHOR OR THE PUBLISHER.